TABLE OF CONTENTS

INTRODUCTION

"Climate change is destroying our path to sustainability. Ours is a world of looming challenges and increasingly limited resources. Sustainable development offers the best chance to adjust our course." ~Ban K-moon

Aquaponics has been around for a number of centuries already, practiced in China where fish were bred in close proximity to the thriving rice paddies, and by the ancient Aztecs who built floating barges called chinampas in Mexico.

Chinampas were largely a network of canals that supported the growth of various crops on these floating islands. Plant growth was fed and sustained by the nutrient-rich waste material that was at the bottom of these canals.

In China, rice paddies were grown together with a variety of fish that were local to the region.

At this time, they not only made use of fish, but also practiced caging ducks that were suspended in these ponds, where the excrement was used to feed the thriving rice paddies.

The ancient Chinese were the first to practice the art of symbiosis where there was sustainability between ducks, fish and rice that was being grown.

It is thought that this particular technique of agricultural farming with fish began as early as the 5th Century A.D. by Chinese settlers who had brought the concept with them when they migrated from the Yunnan region.

Aquaponics is sometimes referred to as aquaculture and is a marriage between aquaculture and hydroponics.

The main difference between the two is that you are adding fish to the equation and the waste that the fish produce is what is turned into a beneficial bacterium that forms nutrient-rich food for your plants.

In the pages that follow we are going to take a look at how some of these aquaponic systems have changed and developed over the years, and which systems that are currently being built and utilized are not only cost effective, but also successful.

The main aim for anyone getting involved in aquaponics is to look at sustainability and reduce their carbon footprint, as well as make the best use of the resources we currently have at our disposal.

CHAPTER 1: UNDERSTANDING AQUAPONICS IN THE 21ST CENTURY

"Just one square meter gives you more yield that in one acre of land. That's an ideal system for a developing country. [It] will produce up to 300 cucumbers a year… A system like that can supply a family with fresh vegetables and with minerals and also with protein." ~Dr. Nick Sadiov, aquaponics researcher and leader at the Aquaculture Centre of Excellence in Lethbridge

The secret to successful aquaponics is being able to combine the art of hydroponics and aquaculture.

Hydroponics is where you can successfully grow a wide variety of plants, vegetables, herbs and even flowering plants in a soil-less environment, making use of very little water.

In hydroponics, much of the work is done by both the water, as well as the circulation of oxygen that reaches the roots of the plants being grown.

One of the biggest differences between the two forms of gardening or farming is that with hydroponics, the nutrient system feeding the plants is already pre-mixed.

This mixture contains all the nutrients needed in the water. The plants make use of all of the nutrients for them to grow to their maximum capacity. Getting this nutrient mix correct can take loads of practice and time.
It can take trial and error resulting in plants suffering from root rot, which is extremely common in hydroponics.

DECIDING WHAT YOU WANT

Your very first step when it comes to setting up your aquaponics system is deciding on what you want.

You should have a clear image or picture in your mind as to what the end result should be.

If you currently have a lot of the equipment necessary to build an Ebb and Flow or Flood and Drain system, and you know that you can upcycle a lot of what you have right now, it doesn't make sense to go out and spend money on setting up another system where you have to purchase all of the necessary components from scratch. Rather, use what you have but invest in those things that are going to make a genuine difference to the success of your system.

This would include investing in a better quality growing medium for your plants and possibly even better quality fish for stocking your setup.

Once you have a clearer idea of the end result you are trying to achieve, you can then begin to put pen to paper and plan the layout of your design.

This could include taking physical measurements so that you are confident that the space that you have available will meet the needs of the system that you are designing.

If not, it will be time to go back to the drawing board and re-measure or redesign so that your plan is workable.

Due to aquaponics becoming more and more popular, it is becoming easier to purchase existing systems either online or via a number of suppliers.

Maybe you are really handy and would enjoy the challenge of physically building your system yourself. Whichever route you plan to take, the single most important factor to consider with aquaponics is patience while waiting for your system to cycle.

Impatience will end up costing you a lot of money in both plants and fish.

SYSTEMS CURRENTLY BEING USED

Aquaculture would incorporate rearing an entire range of aquatic animals, which could include fish, prawns, crayfish and even snails, in a tank-based environment.

When combined with hydroponics, growing plants, vegetables, herbs and even certain flowering cultivars are added. This environment is usually mutually beneficial and much of the growth that takes place is interdependent on one another.

When it comes to nutrients in aquaponics there is no need for any of these pre-mixed solutions that would need to be purchased and added to the water in a hydroponic system. Instead, water from the aquatic system is channeled through to the hydroponic system.

Here the waste-products and excrement from the fish are broken down by bacteria that turn into nitrates.

These nitrates are what are necessary for the plants in the hydroponic component of the system to grow.

Once each of the plants have taken up whatever nitrates and nutrients they need into their root system, the water is recirculated back into the ponds where the fish live.

One of the most interesting parts of beginning an aquaponic journey is that your system can be as large or as small as you want it to be, it's completely up to you.

Aquaponics is becoming increasingly popular and is moving from just being a home-based hobby, where it could be just a smaller system in a basement, in the lounge area or on a kitchen countertop.

Some make use of their patio or invest in larger commercial enterprises fitted to greenhouses.

These commercial aquaponics systems usually contain a number of ponds that have fish at different stages of their lifecycle, or age.

The main reason for this is so that the aquaponic farmer knows which of the fish are ready for breeding, which of the fish are still babies and need more time to grow, and which of the fish are ready for consumption.

Depending on the size of the system, they can range from being fairly simple units, to being extremely complex in nature—although the main purpose is exactly the same.

It mimics and copies a natural aquatic ecosystem that has the plant-based or plant-growing component attached to it.

Instead of making use of a pre-mixed nutrient system, the waste from the fish is broken down by bacteria and recirculated to feed the plants.

While hydroponics focuses solely on the growth of soilless fruit, vegetables, herbs and even flowers, aquaponics incorporates the use of fish to produce the required nutrients for these plants to grow.

Agriculture is being transformed in the 21st century by the incorporation of these two methods of food production and agriculture for a number of reasons:

Whether you are looking at self-reliance and sustainability within your own home, aquaponics is a means that can quite easily support a family with its plant-based food needs, as well as protein in the form of fish.

Our global climate is currently under threat and this is a method of being able to provide renewable resources for homes and larger, commercial-based sustainability.

One such place is The Aquaponics Innovation Center, located in Montello, Wisconsin, which offers extensive training as a college. They are operating from the perspective of a collaborative, private–public venture that conducts state of the art demonstrations and research.

According to their website, in their article entitled, Aquaponics Transforms 21st Century Agriculture (n.d.), there is a massive transformation taking place in the agricultural sector at the moment.

Some of the main reasons for these changes over to aquaponics is because it results in both safe food movement and the food production is sustainable.

The course that they offer is only one semester long, however those who attend qualify for a

They operate with six replicate aquaponics production units that are capable of nutrient film technique (NFT), media and deep water, or raft aquaponic production.

During this training they also cover things that are vital to mastering the art of aquaponics. Some of these include:

- Measurement and manipulation of lighting;
- Entomology (study of insect movements by collecting them, identifying them and monitoring);
- Analysis of water chemistry;
- Analysis of microbiology;
- Purging and quarantine systems;
- Measurement of plant growth and plant physiology; and
- Adaptability of production units.

This gives us a better understanding that aquaponics is being taken seriously as a modern day solution to many agricultural challenges that we face in terms of space availability, climate change, land availability, and our ability to provide healthier food sources that are genuinely organic versus growing crops treated with harmful pesticides and carcinogens that are used on most commercial farms.

WHAT CAN BE GROWN USING YOUR AQUAPONICS SYSTEM

An important consideration when choosing the plants to grow as part of your aquaponic system is whether both the plants and the fish have the same or very similar pH requirements.

It is not just the pH that comes into play with successful aquaponic plants and harvesting, but also the water temperature.

The closer you are able to match these two factors, the more the system will be successful and thrive.

There needs to be close synergy between the two.

An example would be that lettuce, herbs, and certain vegetables do well with warmer fresh water and fish such as Tilapia that thrive in these conditions.

You would need to look at heavily stocking your system if you want success with fruiting plants like peppers and tomatoes.

Of course, similar to its counterpart, hydroponics, there are some plants that do well under any conditions in an aquaponic system, and those are:

ARUGULA:

(*Eruca sativa*) is also known to many as garden rocket, roquette or rucola and is an edible plant that is often added to salads, although it could also be cooked.

Originating from the Mediterranean, it is often used in both French and Italian foods. It has a peppery taste and adds bold flavor to whatever dish it is added to.

Many people choose to make pesto with it. While this is an extremely popular plant to grow in aquaponics, it is recommended that it is grown indoors.

They can easily reach about 15cm in width, making it important to harvest and cut back regularly. From the time that your seedlings start germinating, it takes only about a week to sprout completely.

The benefit of working with Arugula is that you can either harvest the baby flowers and use them in salads, or you can wait until they are fully grown and ready to be harvested.

If you want to improve your harvesting conditions, cut around the center of the plant, leaving the new growth still in place. It is going to take about 55 to 60 days for the plant to reach full maturity.

If the plant begins to taste too peppery, this is an indication that your plant is over-mature.

Some of the benefits of arugula are that they are high in vitamin C, potassium and antioxidants. It is even believed that they can ward off cancer.

BASIL:

Another name for basil is St. Joseph's Wort and it is an herb that belongs to the mint family. It's thought that basil possibly contains anti-inflammatory benefits while being antibacterial as well.

A lesser known fact is that it could possibly assist in fighting off aging. The ideal growing conditions for basil is a pH of between 5.5 to 6.5.

They should ideally be spaced about 20cm apart or with around eight to forty plants per m^2. Average germination takes around a week with a full growth cycle of about five to six weeks.

You can look at harvesting as soon as the plant is about 15cm tall. They do best in a sunny environment where temperatures are around 68°-75°F. While they prefer sunlight, they grow much better in a slightly sheltered environment.

Plants grow to be between 30 and 70cm in height and about 30cm wide.

You can successfully grow basil in media beds, using the Nutrient Film Technique or DWC. Basil is an extremely popular herb to grow in aquaponics and is most successful in Italy.

CHIVES:

Chives belong to the onion family and most aquaponics growers tend to purchase these as seeds, plant them in smaller planters with the right grow medium and within a few days they are already beginning to shoot smaller, brightly colored shoots.

Chives do extremely well in organic matter. You can rely on a germination time of around 5 days.

After the shoots have begun to appear, they are ready to be transplanted into pots that are suitable for the DWC method of aquaponics.
Expanded clay offers great support when it comes to your chives thriving. Full growth takes place between 75 to 90 days, although you should watch your plants closely as this growth cycle could be shortened in an aquaponic environment.

Remember that when you harvest chives, you need to leave approximately an inch from where the roots are, to ensure continuous growth.

KALE:

Kale is one of the easiest vegetables to grow when you are first starting out with aquaponics. It is a member of the cabbage family and is extremely healthy for you to eat as well.

Kale is high in calcium, and vitamins C and K, as well as beta carotene and is also a great antioxidant. Something worth mentioning about kale is that although it doesn't grow very high, as a leafy vegetable it needs quite a bit of space to grow.

You will need to make sure that you have enough space, which may mean only being able to do so in an outdoor system. If you are planning on growing kale, look for one of the varieties that is common to your region because there are many available out there. You stand a much better chance at success if you choose one of these rather than something exotic that doesn't grow very well in your region.

Kale is better suited to growing in the cooler months and usually flourishes early springtime. For kale to survive and thrive it needs to remain moist all the time and the water temperature should be in the region of 55°–70°F. Because it is better suited to cooler temperatures, keeping the air temperature to within the same sort of range as the water temperature shouldn't be a problem.

Kale prefers a pH of between 6.0 – 7.5. Surprisingly it is not a nutrient-demanding plant and can be matched with most fish that are easy to maintain. Koi and tilapia would be ideal.

In an aquaponics system, your kale should be ready to harvest in only six weeks (from seedling to fully grown).

If you are planting seeds, this process will take a little longer.

There are loads of benefits to considering kale with your aquaponics crop but one of the most important of these is that they are easy to maintain and highly nutritious.

LEAFY LETTUCE:

This is one of the most successful of all leafy green vegetables that can be grown in an aquaponics system because the lettuce plant thrives in water.

The most successful water temperature to grow lettuce would be between 70° and 74°F. If you are only starting out with aquaponics as a beginner, lettuce is a great choice of vegetables to begin with.

It's also recommended that you start your lettuce off from seedlings, rather than from planting the seeds yourself.

If you do decide to plant your own seeds, make sure that these are planted in a germinating tray and once the plants are big enough, carefully transplant them over to your aquaponics system.

Lettuce grows best in media bed, DWC and NFT systems. They require an ideal pH of between 6.0 and 7.0.

Lettuce begins flowering only once the temperature reaches over 75°F. While lettuce generally prefers full sunlight, they enjoy light shade when the weather is warmer than usual.

At full growth, you can expect your lettuce to be about 20 to 30 cm in height, and anywhere between 25 - 35 cm in width.

The average growing time for lettuce is around 24 to 32 days, this could be longer depending on the variety you are growing. It normally takes lettuce about 3 to 7 days to germinate.

Part of the reasons why lettuce do so well in aquaponics is because of the levels of nutrients in the water produced by the fish.

While we have mainly mentioned leafy lettuce here, there are a variety of lettuce that are especially popular when it comes to being grown in an aquaponic environment.

These are iceberg lettuce which are better suited to cooler climates than warmer temperatures; butterhead lettuce that is a popular variety for adding to salads all over the world.

Romaine lettuce grows in an upright fashion and the leaves are quite tightly folded over. This variety of lettuce is slow to bolt and tastes sweet.

The final type of lettuce is the first that we have mentioned here, leafy lettuce. Because lettuce is always in such high demand, it is great to consider as a commercial crop or commercial venture.

Lettuce is a winter crop and does much better in cooler climates.

The pH levels need to be closely monitored when it comes to growing lettuce so that the lettuce doesn't display signs of nutrient deficiency.

Seedlings can be transplanted within a few weeks as soon as they have about two to three leaves.

If you supplement with phosphorus fertilizers as well as exposing them to direct sunlight for a few days before transplanting usually results in the plants becoming hardier and their survival rate is higher.

If you want crisp lettuce, you need to grow your plants at a rapid rate making sure that the plants receive all of the nutrients required for them to grow, keeping pH and temperatures at the levels necessary for the crop to thrive.

You can look at harvesting your lettuce as soon as the heads are big enough to eat.

If you are growing lettuce commercially, they should be harvested as soon as the heads reach an average weight of between 250g to 400g.

The secret to harvesting lies in harvesting your lettuce as early in the morning as possible and then chilling the heads.

MINT:

Mint can be grown using an aquaponic system but because it grows so quickly and prolifically, it is one of those herbs that should be avoided.

It is extremely difficult to control once it starts growing and you run the risk of choking out your system.

One of the other major reasons why mint is not a great idea for aquaponics is that it is likely to take over any of your other plants, making it impossible for them to thrive.

MOST HOUSE PLANTS:

You could successfully plant and grow most house plants in an aquaponic system as long as you stick to the rules regarding matching the pH requirements of the plants to the fish that you are wanting to stock.

The air temperature also needs to be factored in so that you can decide whether to grow your plants indoors, in a greenhouse or outdoors.

There are a large variety of houseplants that can be successfully grown, especially edible houseplants such as nasturtium.

Sunflowers grow really well, although with these they do need support as the top of the flowers are really heavy.

You can also consider the brightly colored tulips, but these would need to be rooted first because the bulbs don't like to be fully submerged in water.

Once these have taken root though, they are good to go.

Tulips prefer cooler temperatures initially – 60°F but, once they are growing, their temperature requirements jump to 70°F.

An excellent solution to this cool and warm requirement is to keep the bulbs in a refrigerator for approximately two weeks while they are rooting and then place the shooting bulbs into a flood and drain system with fish that can withstand the temperature range of between 60°–75°F.

Other flowering plants that do really well are roses, marigolds, and water hyacinth.

WATERCRESS:

Watercress is another vegetable that you may want to consider growing as a beginner because it multiplies so easily.

This could also be challenging though because if not controlled it can cause problems with your grow bed, causing it to become clogged.

By only planting a single, small plant, it will multiply at a rapid rate.

If you are planning on growing your watercress from seeds the best way would be to add the seeds to the top of your growing media, you would do this in a similar way that you would plant them in conventional soil, but remember that this is a soil-less growing method.

Watercress can be cultivated from cuttings if this is going to be easier for you —all that you would need to do would be to sprinkle the cuttings across the tray instead.

Place each of the trays gently into the water and wait for them to grow. Because they grow so quickly, you may want to keep some of the cuttings or seedlings from the best watercress to be used for propagation at a later stage.

The following plants require a great deal more nutrients and will usually only do well in an aquaponics system that is well established and heavily stocked.

CUCUMBERS:

Depending on the variety of cucumber you are planning to grow, the average spacing should be between 30cm to 60cm apart or between two to five plants per m^2. They need a pH of between 5.5 to 6.5. It only takes them between three to seven days to germinate, but the germination temperature should be around 20° to 30^oC. Total growing time is between 55 to 65 days at a temperature that ranges between 71° to 82^oF. Notice how cucumbers have quite a high tolerance for temperature fluctuations. The evening temperatures can go as low as 64^oF, but your plants must be protected from frost at all cost. They thrive in a fully sunny environment. When harvesting, your plant height should be about 20cm to 200cm tall and 20cm to 80cm wide.

Cucumbers are best grown using the DWC method or in media beds. A benefit of growing cucumbers is that you can grow them along with other members of the same family, including squash, melons and zucchinis.

They are a summer crop. Part of the reason that they are suited to growing in media beds is because they have a longer and larger root structure.

Although you could try and grow them in a raft-based system, the roots could potentially block, or clog filters, creating further problems down the line.

They need a lot of nutrients and potassium and this should be factored in when planning on stocking your fish.

Cucumbers love humidity and so consider growing these if your climate supports these types of conditions.

Watch for problems if your temperatures drop below 50^oF because your plants are going to stop growing at that time.

You can transplant your seedlings after two weeks and once they have between four to five true leaves.

Be aware that these plants grow very quickly, and it is a great habit to get into to cut certain tips when the stem is about two meters long to remove lateral branches.

This will also give the plant better ventilation. Other plants can be secured by leaving only two buds that are furthest apart from one another that are coming from the same stem.

Cucumbers also need a support structure for them to grow properly as this also gives them necessary aeration. Cucumbers could be susceptible to a number of problems like powdery mildew and grey mold—be on the lookout for any of these diseases and treat with natural methods as we have already discussed.

In ideal conditions one cucumber plant can be harvested between 10 to 15 times. It's also important to make sure that you harvest every few days so that the plants don't become too large and so that you can allow the others along the same plant to grow.

BROCCOLI:

The ideal time to grow broccoli is in the winter. It's recommended that the media bed method is used.

Please note that this is quite a difficult vegetable to grow because it doesn't like warm temperatures at all. When you are growing your broccoli, make sure that your pH is between 6.0 and 7.0.

Average temperatures during the day should be between 55° to 64°F, which you can see is a lot cooler than most of the other vegetables we have spoken about here.

Although they prefer a cooler climate, they enjoy full sun and can endure some shade. If they are in the shade all the time though, they will grow much slower.

When growing broccoli, the average spacing between your plants should be between 40 to 70cm or approximately three to five plants per m^2.

It should take your broccoli about five to six days to germinate at an average temperature of 77°F. You will notice that the plants need a much higher temperature for germination than actual growth. The full growth cycle is anywhere between 60 to 100 days from being transplanted.

You can harvest your crop once the height reaches 30 to 60cm and the width reaches the same: 30cm to 60cm.

I mentioned above that the seedlings take about a week to germinate. Once they have germinated, it's time to transplant them into your media bed.

This should be done once there are about four to five true leaves on the plants and they are about 15cm to 20cm tall.

Getting the spacing correct when transplanting the seedlings is important, otherwise their growth will be stunted.

When harvesting your broccoli, the buds of the heads need to be both firm and tight.

If you notice that the buds are beginning to separate from one another, or they are beginning to flower, make sure that you harvest immediately.

PEAS AND BEANS:

Both peas and beans can be grown in aquaponics. The climbing varieties are recommended because they take up less space than normal beans and peas do.

The yield for the climbing varieties is also two to three times greater than normal. The pH for both varieties range between 5.5 to 7.0 and ideal temperatures are between 71° to 79°F during the day and a minimum of between 61° to 64°F at night.

Both plants enjoy full sun and should be grown in either summer or autumn, depending on the cultivars.

It is recommended that the media bed aquaponic technique is used to grow these. Consider spacing your plants between ten to thirty centimeters depending on the variety, with bush varieties having between twenty to forty plants per m^2 and approximately only ten to twelve climbing plants per m^2.

Depending on the variety and cultivar, growing time can take anything between 50 to 110 days to reach full maturity. By this time, the plant would have reached a height of about 60cm, with a width of about 250cm for a climbing plant.

The normal bush variety will have a height of about 60cm and a width of about 80cm.

If you are planning on growing beans and peas you can place your seeds directly into the grow media beds about four centimeters deep, making sure that the water level will be high enough during germination.

This process usually takes about eight to ten days and the temperature necessary for correct germination is between 70° to 79°F.

Because they are extremely difficult to transplant successfully, any supporting equipment needs to be in place before or at the time of planting your seedlings.

Special care should be taken to watch out for spiders and other aphids that are fairly common with beans and peas.

Wherever possible avoid planting companion plants or pay close attention to what you plan to plant with them to avoid contamination of these diseases.

When harvesting snap beans, the pods should be crisp when harvesting, with the inside seeds being small or undeveloped.

To harvest successfully, remove the pod by holding the stem in one hand and the pod in the other. This will allow for further growth at a later stage.

When harvesting shell beans, the pods should be picked as soon as they change color. The pods should be plump. Try not to leave these on the plant for too long as this affects the quality of the beans.

For dry beans, the opposite is the case. The shells or pods should be left to dry as much as possible.
 This makes harvesting easier as the pods split open easier when they are dry.

PEPPERS:

While it is difficult to grow peppers in a conventional gardening system because they require plenty of sunshine and are very particular about the water they use, they are suited to smaller indoor aquaponics systems. The reason for this is because you can control the temperature to exactly meet their specific needs.

A Deep-Water Culture (DWC) method of growing peppers is not suitable—they do much better using a "flood and drain" technique (more about each of these systems in the following chapter).

There are four main genus of peppers which will help you to understand which is going to best suit your needs—whether you are after the Capsicum, Pimenta, Piper, or Red pepper, the important consideration is that they all have exactly the same needs and requirements for growth in aquaponics. Before you begin to grow peppers, the single most important thing to do is to decide which of the above four peppers you are wanting to grow. If you are only starting off with aquaponics, it is highly recommended that you begin with the conventional bell pepper.

Peppers enjoy warm temperatures, which is why many people prefer to grow them in greenhouses. You may want to build a trellis that would aid your peppers to flourish in your aquaponic system.

The water temperature for peppers should be a minimum of 60°F to 70°F, although this can go even as high as 75°F. Beware of water temperatures exceeding 80°F as this will cause your peppers to become deformed. As a side note—the hotter the pepper, the warmer the water requirement.

Air temperature is as important as water temperature and this should be between 70°F – 90°F.

The ideal water pH should be between 5.5 and 6.5 but peppers can thrive in pH as high as 7.0.

Peppers need a lot of sunshine and a warmer climate. If you live in a moderate climate and you plan to grow peppers, you may consider growing them in a greenhouse instead.

I mentioned earlier that you may wish to build a trellis to support your pepper plants. This is because peppers can grow between one and three feet tall and the same width. It's important to note that the leaves of the peppers hang over the to protect them from direct sunlight.

SWISS CHARD:

This is a hugely popular aquaponically grown plant. It can also be grown using all aquaponic methods, i.e. NFT, DWC and grow beds. The recommended pH for swiss chard is between 6.0 to 7.5 and prefers temperatures of between 61° to 75°F. Ideal growing conditions are in full sun, although when temperatures exceed 79°F, the plants will need to be moved into partial shading. When planting swiss chard, make sure that you leave spacing about 30cm x 30cm apart, or plat between 15 to 20 plants in a m^2 area.

It takes about 30 to 35 days for your plants to fully mature and be ready for harvesting. This should normally be grown in late winter or early spring. Something to be aware of when growing swiss chard from seedlings is that they grow more than one plant per seed and so you may need to thin your crop out from time to time. You can easily achieve this by removing older leaves that will also encourage new growth with your plant.

The right height for harvesting is around 30 to 60cm, with a width of around 30 to 40cm.

A major benefit of swiss chard is that you can continuously harvest your plants. As you cut off the plants that are being harvested, this will encourage new growth and new leaves will begin to grow and the cycle continues. The only recommendation when it comes to harvesting is to avoid damaging the central growing point when you are harvesting your crop. Otherwise the next new leaves will battle to grow.

TOMATOES:

One of the main reasons why tomatoes do exceptionally well in aquaponics is that you are able to control how much sun the plants get. Surprisingly, they are a popular choice for newcomers to aquaponics, however, they are more difficult to grow than you would imagine at first. It's important to understand the requirements that tomatoes need to grow successfully before you even begin to consider this particular crop. Tomatoes not only have specific needs in aquaponics, but there is also a special way that they need to be tended to. Because the tomato is actually a berry and not a vegetable, but rather a fruit. Originally from South America, you would then understand why it prefers a warmer climate to other vegetables. A lot of nutrient-rich water is also necessary for your tomatoes to grow successfully. Temperatures should range between 65° to 85°F, but they will stop growing if it is warmer than 95°F. As a matter of interest, if the evening temperatures are higher than 85°F, the tomatoes will not turn red at all.

Although your tomatoes need a constant supply of water, they also need to be drained. Keeping tomato plants submerged constantly will cause the crop to fail.

The water pH needs to be between 5.5 and 6.5 for tomatoes and so the best possible fish to match to these pH levels would be Tilapia, Koi, Crappie, Goldfish, Angelfish and as a last resort, possibly Trout (remember that trout prefer cooler water temperatures).

Tomato plants need sufficient space between them, with enough support for them to be able to grow upwards unencumbered. Your crop could grow anywhere between two feet to six feet in height and so when you are initially setting up your tomato system, make sure that they are placed at least two feet apart from one another.

Watch potassium levels in your system. While they require plenty of nitrogen during their early stages of development, this requirement quickly turns to needing more potassium to make sure that the fruit forms correctly. To keep your tomato plants thriving, you need to trim them once they reach approximately two feet in height. You may also want to remove some of the leaves from the bottom of the plant as this will help the nitrogen flow from the stems to the fruit, allowing them to grow bigger quicker.

On average, you could expect anywhere from 25 to 35 tomatoes per plant, variety dependent of course. They grow quickly and you should be able to see growth over a two-week period, with fully developed flowers around four weeks. You can plan to harvest your tomatoes within eight weeks of planting.

There has been success in growing the following crops under highly monitored and regulated environments:

Bananas, Beets, Carrots, Dwarf citrus trees: lemons, limes, and oranges, Dwarf pomegranate trees, Edible flowers: nasturtiums, violas, and orchids. Also: Microgreens, including Onions, Radishes and Sweet corn.

BENEFITS OF GROWING YOUR OWN FRUIT, VEGETABLES, HERBS AND FISH USING AQUAPONICS

Some of the most important benefits of being able to grow your own fruit, vegetables, herbs and fish are listed below:

- The biggest advantage of making use of aquaponics is that it takes an environmentally friendly stance towards saving the planet. Because it mimics the natural ecosystem, it makes use of very little water and also limited to no power at all (unless you are running heaters or filters in your pond setup. If you are using a normal aquarium with ornamental fish, then you would use whatever amount of water your tank would require. You would only need to top up water from time to time to keep your aquarium levels stable. This would also be an indication of whatever water your plants would use to grow.
- For me it is all about sustainability and becoming self-reliant. A good aquaponic system would easily be able to support a family of between four to six people continuously once it is up and running and maintained correctly. Larger systems would be suitable for commercial farming and could even feed communities in regions where it is not viable for an entire farming setup to be established.
- The start up costs are fairly low. This would definitely prove a cost saving at the end of the day. Because there are not costly premixed nutrients required in your aquaponic system, your only real costs are your fish food (when required) and the cost of your initial set up. If you are looking at designing a commercial aquaponic system then you can expect your costs to be higher than a home-based system, but you would still save on heavy commercial farming equipment, pesticides, labor and many other cost factors that commercial farmers face daily.
- You may even currently have a fish tank in your home right now that could be converted into an aquaponic system for a reasonable price. It's worth mentioning that a fish tank can only support smaller ornamental fish with limited stocking capacity. The moment you are looking at bigger fish such as Koi or Tilapia, you would need to consider larger tanks and bigger systems.
- Because aquaponics operates as a closed recirculating system, there is little to no water that is lost throughout the growing process. This makes it by far the most economical way to grow food in a cost-effective way.
- Your initial outlay is extremely small because you only need to consider your fish, the food that they eat and water, as well as either seeds or seedlings of the crop that you are planning to grow.
- A huge plus factor is that aquaponics really is completely organic. There are no

synthetic, premix additives, pesticides and chemicals that need to go into growing the vegetables and fish of your choice.

- While some of your fish could be picky eaters and you will need to buy them their own food, but remember that whatever you are feeding them will eventually feed you and their pellets are going to turn into protein that you would eventually consume. It makes sense then that you feed your fish the very best food available, that matches their specific needs. Naturally this is for the larger edible variety of fish versus ornamentals.
- Due to the nature of this type of farming many of the plant varieties are easy to grow and the growing time is drastically reduced. This means that harvesting takes place a lot earlier. In some instances, it is said that growing times can be shortened up to six times the average growing time required under commercial growing circumstances.
- While this can support individual families with their food requirements, including protein (contained in the fish), when one considers this type of farming on a larger, commercial scale, entire communities can become fully sustainable. It is recommended that you consider the size and scale of the system that best suits your particular needs. Also take into account exactly what crops you are going to eat. There's no point in growing cabbage if it's a vegetable that none of your family ever eats.
- The amount of space required for a full ecosystem is a lot smaller than conventional agriculture and it is suited for indoors, on patios, in greenhouses and areas that have space limitations.
- You are not limited by any one specific crop as you can produce a variety of different vegetables simultaneously, as long as the temperature and pH of the crop and fish match.
- Should you ever reach an overstocking system with your fish, there is also a market for them to be sold to other aquaponics enthusiasts.
- It's an important benefit that you can grow at the source—that means that you can harvest and eat immediately without your crop having to be frozen, stored, or injected with various hormones to keep them fresh to be transported to your local convenience store. The nutrient benefits of this in itself are huge as you are getting all of the goodness that nature intended.
- One final benefit that I can think of to mention here would be that there are limited diseases in aquaponics, opposed to hydroponics where many of the plants are highly susceptible to root rot.

CHAPTER 2: DIFFERENT AQUAPONIC SYSTEMS

" Recirculating aquaponic and hydroponic farms are sustainable options that can have controlled inputs and known outputs, like other existing organic farms. In fact, many recirculating farms not only meet, but can exceed current organic standards. They can be eco-efficient and have versatile designs and reduced use of water, fossil fuels, fertilizers and electricity. " ~ Marianne Cufone, Executive Director of the Recirculating Farms Coalition

The three most important decisions that you need to make before you decide which system is going to work best for you is to:

1. Decide which system is going to work best for you?
2. Obtain all of the necessary components required to construct the system, and
3. Put it all together!

Every single aquaponics system needs the following to be effective:

- An aquarium, tank or pond for the fish.
- A grow bed for the plants.
- A means of transporting water both to the plants and the fish and back again (a recirculating system). Most people find that a pump of some description works best.
- A means of draining the water from the grow bed back to the aquarium, tank or pond where the fish are, siphon type pipes are often used to serve this purpose.

There are three main different types of aquaponics systems: Deep Water Culture (DWC), Nutrient Film Bed (NFT), and Media Bed. While these are certainly not the only aquaponics systems available, they are the three that we are going to focus on because they are the most common.

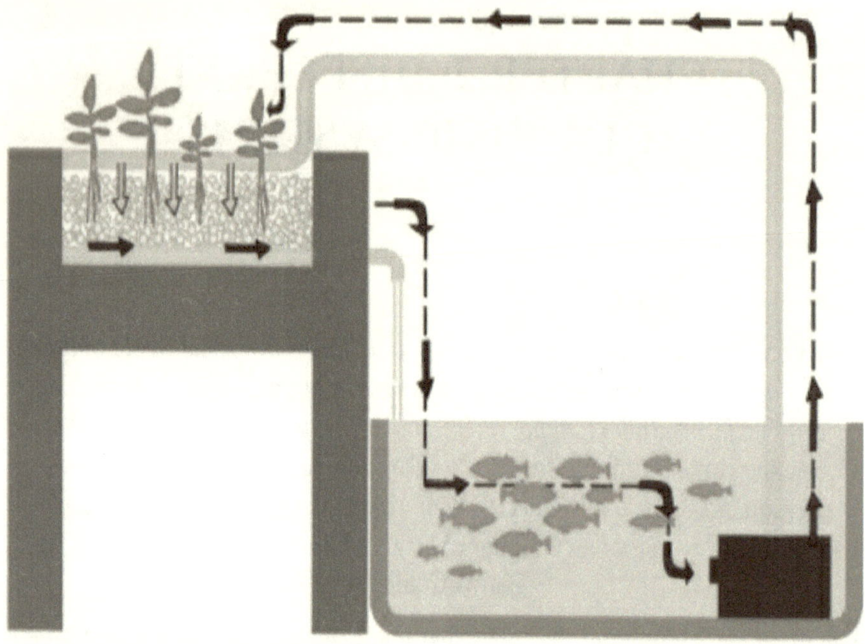

aquaponic system

A Typical Aquaponic System

Before beginning with your design or deciding on what system you are planning on using, it is important that you consider the end use of your system and ask several questions that can help you make the best decision possible. Are you planning on only building your system as a means of supporting your household with some additional organic vegetables all year round? Are you planning on considering a commercial venture with a much larger farm that will grow a large variety of different crops? Are you planning on using your system for educational purposes? Whatever your chief use is going to be, there are a number of other considerations that you need to consider:

These are as follows:

- What is your environment like? Do your seasons fluctuate radically between heat and cold? If this is the case, would it be better for you to consider your system inside versus outside, or in a greenhouse environment where it can be protected by some of the natural elements?

- How much space do you have available to you? This will also directly impact your decision on how much you will be able to produce and where. There is no point in looking to begin a commercial venture, when you live in a small 2-bedroom tenement building (unless you convince the landlord to allow you to convert and utilize the entire roof area, which could then provide food year round for all the tenants).

- What are you planning on growing—as a sidebar, there really is no point growing fruits or vegetables that you do not eat. This will naturally be a waste. It is the same as stocking the fish that you do not find palatable to the taste. All that will happen is that these will go to waste and that is the complete contradiction to this type of sustainable farming.

- Consider the different technical capacity and capabilities that you have. Some systems are pretty straightforward to put together and you would be able to manage on your own, while others require a slightly more professional approach. Make sure that you understand how your system works, what can go wrong, how to correct it if it does go wrong and how to maintain the system. Remember that when your system is faulty your fish and your crop are at risk. Initial close monitoring of a number of factors are important to the success of whatever system you choose to use.

DEEP WATER CULTURE (DWC):

Deep Water Culture Aquaponics, also known as (DWC):

Closely modeled after the same principles that the ancient Aztecs and Chinese cultures used, this method is really just a modernized version. As the saying goes, "if it ain't broke, don't try and fix it!" This method has been used for hundreds of years successfully, so it has been a natural progression to duplicate this method today with a couple of modern tweaks. This method of aquaponics is really low maintenance and is best suited for fruits, vegetables and herbs that grow rapidly. Examples of these would include leafy greens and lettuce. The setup costs for this system are also reasonable, so you won't break the bank if you decide that this addictive hobby is not for you.

Once you understand how a deep-water culture design works, you will find it easy to adapt and design your own system that will meet the demands of your crops, your fish, your water, your pH and temperatures. Being able to monitor these will literally provide you with all that you need to run a successful aquaponics system.

Understanding that the DWC is very similar to the other systems, in that they still need to be monitored to make sure that both the fish and the plants are healthy and that the main ingredient, bacteria cycling, is necessary before starting your system. In any aquaponic system, the crucial ingredient to the success of the system is that the bacteria colony needs to be established before you "cycle" or let your system "go live". In a DWC system the roots of the plants remain submerged all the time or are mostly submerged all the time. Unlike hydroponics where premix nutrients are added to meet the needs of the plants being cultivated, here, the bacteria, fish, pH, water temperature and air temperature factor into the growing cycle and are the only things that need to be monitored closely for the first month that the system is up and running.

While some people use lightweight pots for their plants, the pots of choice are called net pots and are a popular choice for this method.

DWC is also an extremely popular choice for hydroponics. Although the main difference in using it with aquaponics is that you don't need to include grow media. The simplicity of this system is that the floatation device or beds are literally on top of where the fish are and there should be some form of aeration system included.

The design variations are only limited by how far your imagination can stretch, so grab your pen and paper and start thinking about the following:

- How much space do I have available?
- What crops am I planning on cultivating and how will this impact my system?
- With the crops I would like to cultivate, which fish are closely aligned to the temperatures and pH required to sustain optimal growth?
- What is my budget?

Once you have all the answers to the above questions, the next thing would be to physically measure out your system according to your plan. Remember that your system is a recirculating system and so all plumbing components need to be able to move the water between the plants floating in the net pots and back to the fish. (In the following chapter we will go through the nutrient cycle. This will give you a better idea of how the plants receive nutrients from the waste products of the fish).

If you would like to consider a canal system, the tank housing the fish is separate from where the plants are grown, while water is being pumped between the different areas where the plant beds are floating in the water. While this system is a little more intricate and involved it is also more effective as the water is circulated between the plants better.

BUILDING YOUR DWC SYSTEM

If this is the system that you have decided to build, then you are going to need the following:

Aeration:

I mentioned aeration above—it is important that oxygen is added to the water, irrespective of the system you design or choose to make use of. In aquaponics, this is referred to as dissolved oxygen or (DO). This is a vital ingredient to the growth and health of your plants and fish. You can increase the aeration in your system through a number of different methods. Whether you would like to look at diffusers, air stones, air pumps, helping to improve on the DO is something that needs to be monitored closely as it affects both plant and fish.

Biofilter:

Next you will need something called a biofilter. This is where the bacteria go to work to turn the waste produced by the fish into nutrients that are suitable to feed the plants. This process is known as the nitrification process. It is also this process that replaces the chemical premix that would typically be used in a hydroponic system.

Canals:

While we refer to these as canals, what they actually are in a recirculating system is a series of pipes (like large plumbing pipes) or trenches that transport and hold the water pushed through the various tanks by the pumps. Each of these pipes or trenches have holes in them that support the net pots so that they are "floating" in the nutrient enriched water. Depending on how you set up your system, you can add more pipes or trenches to your canals as your planting requirements grow. This could be as a result of your current cultivars growing and needing more space, or it could be that you are planning on adding additional herbs, vegetables, or plants to your system.

Conventional Filter:

A conventional filtration system that is able to filter out anything else that could get into the system. Some prefer screens, reverse osmosis, or even swirl filters to complete this process. The last thing that you want is for the system to become clogged up with leaves or anything that cannot be processed by the biofilter into nutrients to feed the plants.

If you are planning on building a canal system, you will definitely need a pump to help force the water from the fish tanks through the filters and to each of the canals where the plants are floating on the "rafts". Remember that the secret to aquaponics is to keep the water recirculating and moving at all times for the plants to be aerated with the nutrients to help them grow. When choosing your pump, take the size of your tanks into consideration.

Grow Beds – Floating:

These are usually manufactured from a lightweight substance that is able to float easily, that can also support your net pots. In most instances these allow for only the roots to be exposed to the water. The net pots provide the plants the necessary support that they need to grow.

Tank:

A tank for your fish. This can be as large or as small as you require but remember that it needs to meet the needs of the breed or type of fish that you plan to stock. Your fish need to be comfortable and have sufficient space to grow. Some people prefer to have separate tanks that will accommodate their hatchling or fingerling fish (those that are still really small). This is a great idea because it prevents them from becoming food for larger fish, especially if the more mature fish are carnivorous. This tank will be home to them until they become large enough to be moved over. Your tanks will also become the collection point for the waste product that your fish produce.

IMPORTANT TIPS FOR DWC AQUAPONICS

Some important things to take into consideration when it comes to DWC aquaponics are to ensure that there is enough dissolved oxygen in the water. This is achieved with air stones, or pumps. You will need to monitor this regularly to ensure that your plants and fish are healthy and thriving. Without dissolved oxygen, neither your fish nor your plants can survive.

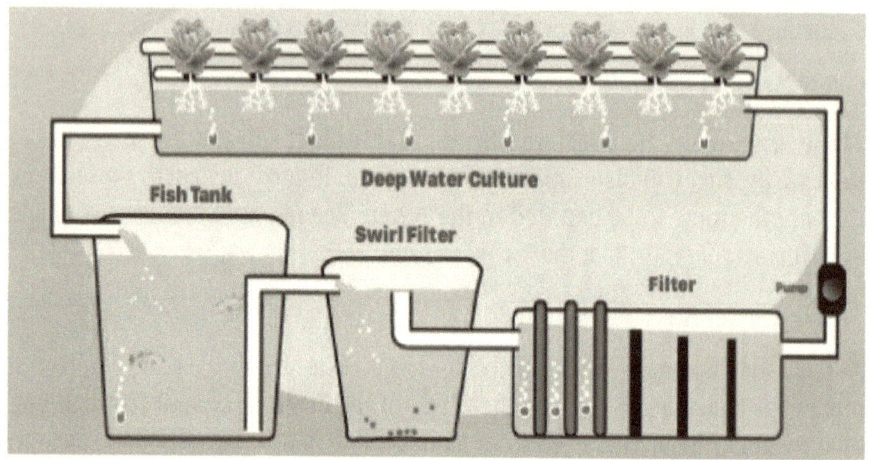

Deep Water Culture System

Remember to monitor your water temperature and pH levels constantly. These need to be in range to match the fish that you have stocked, as well as the plants that you are growing. Also make sure that your nitrification process is happening correctly. (We will discuss this in greater detail in the next chapter).

Check all of your filters, pumps and piping on a regular basis to make sure that there are no blockages so that your water flow is not restricted in any way.

If you are planning on adding any plants to the fish tank, make sure that these are easy to maintain and aren't likely to cause disease for your fish.

Because this system is relatively easy to setup, with costs that can be controlled on the basis of your design, it is ideal for someone who is first starting out with Aquaponics.

FLOOD AND DRAIN OR EBB AND FLOW SYSTEM

This system is by far the most popular system for beginners because it is easy to build and results in fairly good yields for someone who is just starting out.

This system works as follows:

- The plants or grow beds are situated above the aquarium, allowing drainage to take place naturally via the force of gravitation.
- Typically, plants would be planted in a grow medium such as clay pebbles. These will support the roots of the plant and will substitute soil.
- Water from the aquarium or fish tank is pumped into the grow beds by means of a submersible pump.
- The amount of water being pumped into the grow bed is usually monitored with a timer that is turned on and off. This allows for initial flooding and then draining back into the fish tank.
- An automatic timer is placed to control the flood and drain cycle. This makes use of a bell siphon, which means that it operates without electricity.
- The average timing for flooding would be around fifteen minutes per cycle, with a drain cycle of forty-five minutes.

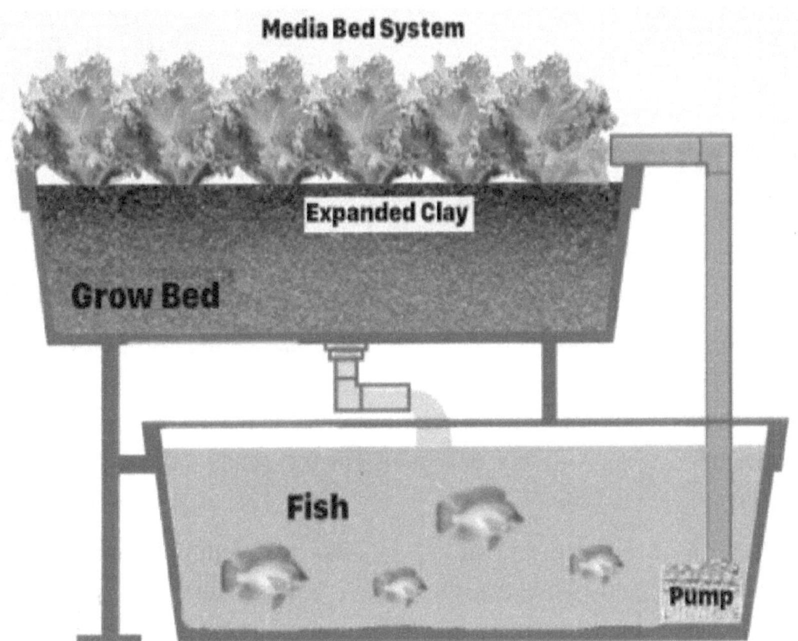

Flood and Drain or Ebb and Flow Technique

NUTRIENT FILM TECHNIQUE (NFT):

While this system is very similar to the DWC method, the difference between the two is that the roots of the plants are watered by a steady flow of water in much smaller volumes. This is why they call it the 'film' technique. The nutrient filled water virtually only moistens the plants root system, but it is constant.

Again, each of the plants sit in net pots in each of the channels or closed recirculating systems while the roots are fed as the water containing all of the nutrients passes by the bottom of the plants, also known as the root zone.

Just like the DWC method, there is constant flow between the different components. The water from the fish tank, pond, or aquarium is pumped into the NFT channel, where the roots are lightly covered, and this water then returns to the fish tank. With each of these systems a separate biofilter is needed.

NFT is one of the best choices when it comes to larger commercial farming. If you are planning on starting out with aquaponics for the first time—the Ebb and Flow system is better suited.

NFT Nutrient Film Technique Aquaponics

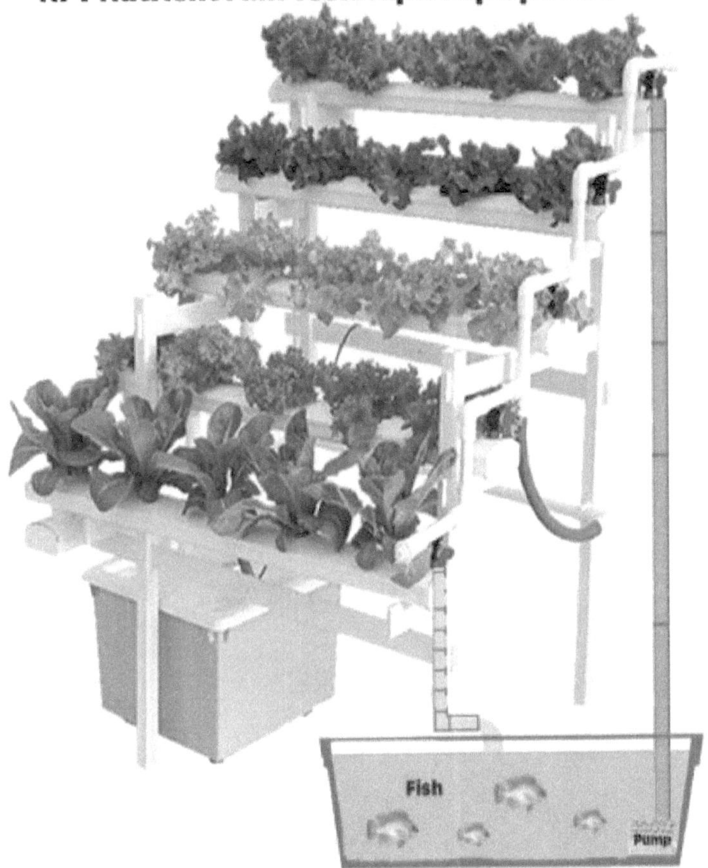

Nutrient Film Technique or NFT

CHAPTER 3: UNDERSTANDING THE NUTRIENT CYCLE

"[Plants] grow extremely rapidly because they have all the nutrients and water they need. It's much better than field production because in the soil, you have insects and not enough water or nutrients." ~ Dr. James Rakocy, "Father of Aquaponics," and former professor at the University of the Virgin Islands

The Aquaponics Cycle

1. Fish - Produce waste

2. Microbes & Worms Convert the waste to feed the plants

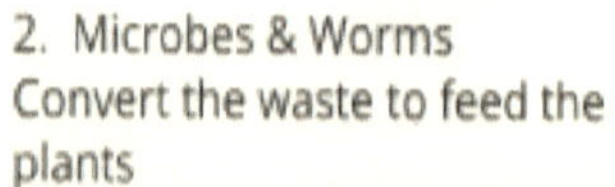

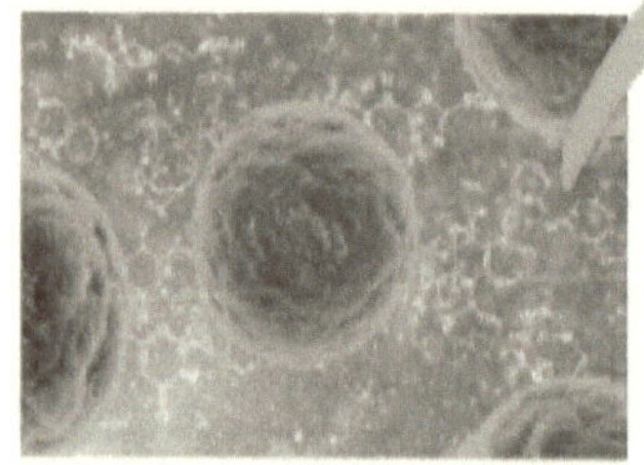

3. Plants - filter the water to return to the fish in a clean state.

UNDERSTANDING THE IMPORTANCE OF THE NUTRIENT CYCLE:

Most aquaponics enthusiasts are impatient and want their system up and running as soon as possible. Before you can, or should get your system going, it should be cycled correctly.

When fish create waste as a byproduct, ammonia and nitrates are created which can be poisonous to the fish and pH levels in the water can also increase.

You can cycle your aquaponics system with your fish or without your fish. I'm going to share both methods with you.

When we refer to "cycling" it's not riding a bicycle—it's ensuring that your beneficial bacteria system that you need for your aquarium, pond or tank are up and running correctly and are effectively changing the harmful nitrates to beneficial nitrites.

The good news is that you can do it with your fish or without fish.

The ideal is to do it fishless because it could potentially save you a lot of money in fish if you happen to get it wrong!

UNDERSTANDING THE ROLE THAT NITROGEN PLAYS IN AQUAPONICS

Nitrogen is crucial for all living organisms. It's what keeps us alive, but at the same time keeps all other living organisms alive as well.

The drawback of nitrogen is that in many different ecosystems there is limited supply of nitrogen present. There are different forms of nitrogen available.

These include atmospheric nitrogen (N2), ammonia (NH3), nitrate (NO3-) and nitrite (NO2-). Animals excrete nitrogenous waste in the form of ammonia, while plants require nitrogen in the form of nitrates to survive. Because plants absorb nitrogen in the form of nitrates and convert this to atmospheric nitrogen (N2), in the ecological system continues to be recycled.

CYCLING YOUR SYSTEM IN THREE EASY STEPS:

Add water to your aquarium tank, or pond and turn on your pump, allowing it to run for two days.

This will dissolve any chlorine from tap water that may be present. Whatever you do, don't add any fish or plants at this stage.

Once this process is complete it's time to add a couple of smaller, cheap fish that you are possibly prepared to lose, think of something like a couple of goldfish.

The purpose of adding these fish to the tank at this point is for them to produce waste which will contain ammonia.

Wait at least two weeks before adding some seedlings to your grow beds.

For the next ten to fifteen days it's important that you don't feed your fish, as this will only create problems for your system.

Don't worry too much, fish can survive for as long as three weeks without food.

At this stage the ammonia levels will be high because the beneficial bacteria required to turn this into nitrites haven't become sufficiently established to begin the nitrogen cycle as yet.

Remember the two nitrifying bacteria — nitrosomonas (NO2), and nitrospira, which converts the nitrite into nitrate. It is this nitrate which is required by the plants as nutrients.

This type of nitrate is beneficial to both plants and fish and is the final step in the nitrogen cycle.

So how do you tell if your system is ready?

You will be able to confirm that your system is now ready as soon as you find nitrates in the water; your water will test with both nitrites and ammonia levels lower than 0.5ppm, and regular feeding will not increase nitrite or ammonia levels.

The ideal should be zero or less than 1mg/liter of ammonia and nitrites in your water within 40 to 50 days. At this stage the nitrate level should be higher than 100ppm.

You can now slowly begin to add more fish to your system, although only a few at a time with a couple of days in between.

The main reason for this is that even though your biofilter is ready and functioning, it needs to populate and grow at the same rate to support your fish.

This would happen quickly in a fully cycled system, but you need to remember that this is still taking place and you don't want to run the risk of losing your fish at this time.

You can begin to add plants at the same time as you begin to cycle your tank, aquarium or pond.

Plants are helpful in absorbing nitrogen from ammonia nitrates and nitrites throughout the cycling process.

Your plants will definitely be happiest once the biofilter is fully established and nitrates are available from the beneficial bacteria and the cycle is 100% complete.

As soon as you have added your plants, they will begin to take root in your new system. You may initially notice some of them turning yellow or dropping a couple of leaves here and there.

This is completely normal. You will not begin to see normal growth in the next couple of weeks. Part of the reason for adding plants at the beginning of the cycling process is that it allows them to catch up with the rooting process and makes sure that they are ready to start absorbing the nutrient-rich fish waste from the system as soon as it becomes available.

MONITORING YOUR CYCLING PROCESS

The full cycling process normally takes anywhere upwards of four to six weeks to complete.

 Knowing this will give you a much better understanding of where in the cycle you are as you move forward.

 You will know that you need to have monitored your pH, nitrite, nitrate and ammonia levels to make sure that each of these are within range.

 If not, you know what to do to correct it. While this entire process is fascinating to watch, unfortunately the only way that you get to see it properly is via a test kit.

 As soon as everything is within the ranges as mentioned above, you can begin to slowly add more fish to your system and the monitoring process that you have had to rigidly follow takes a bit more of a back seat.

 You then get to sit back and do the fun stuff like watching your fish, feeding them and tending to your plants.

Remember to consider each of the following while you are monitoring your cycling process.

TEMPERATURE:

Both types of microorganisms or bacteria mentioned are living and are altered by temperature.

The ideal temperature range is between 77° to 86°F for them to grow. Should the temperatures be out of these parameters, the levels of dissolved oxygen will be affected, and the bacteria will be unable to process the waste as needed.

PH:

The pH plays a vital role in the nitrification process. pH levels outside of 7.0 will begin negatively influencing bacterial performance. This will become completely restricted and virtually non-existent at 6.0. Ideal ranges for Nitrosomonas are between 7.3 to 7.5 and for Nitrosomonas is between 7.0 and 8.0.

NITRIFICATION:

During the nitrification process, ammonia is transformed into nitrates which can be used by plants.

 These nitrates are what makes up the nutrient-rich water that is pumped from the aquarium, tank or pond to water your plants through whatever method you have chosen.

Nitrification includes two steps involving nitrifying or beneficial bacteria:
1. Ammonia is changed into nitrites (NO_2^-) by bacteria called nitrosomonas.
2. Nitrites are changed into nitrates (NO_3^-) by bacteria called nitrobacter.

The product that results from this transformation, nitrates, can then be absorbed as nutrients by your plants.

CHLORAMINES AND CHLORINES:

It's vital to make sure that all chlorine is neutralized completely before adding any form of bacteria to your tank, aquarium or pond.
 Any chloramines or chlorine that remain is highly toxic to the fish, as well as the nitrifying bacteria (beneficial bacteria).

LIGHT SENSITIVITY:

Nitrifying bacteria are especially sensitive to both ultraviolet and blue light.

This light only causes problems during the cycling process and so you should make sure that all lights are turned off for the duration of this period.

Once your system has cycled through, it is quite safe for you to turn these lights back on.

DISSOLVED OXYGEN (DO) LEVELS:

We have discussed how dissolved oxygen levels can adversely affect both plants and fish, but this comes into play much earlier during the nitrification process, as soon as dissolved levels of oxygen concentrations reach below 2.0 mg/liter.

Hitting this level will not affect the nitrosomonas as much as it will affect beneficial bacteria. Nitrosomonas will increase levels of poisonous nitrates in the water. You can reach maximum nitrification rates at dissolved oxygen concentrations above 80% capacity.

SALINITY:

Also referred to as the salt content, this needs to fluctuate between 0-6 ppt with a specific gravity between 1-1.0038 which is best suited to the growth of the freshwater nitrifying bacteria.

 Adjustments to differing salt levels or content could take between 1-3 days before they start to grow at a rapid rate.

MICRONUTRIENTS:

All nitrifying bacteria require micronutrients.
 The most important of these is phosphorous as this is necessary for Adenosine Triphosphate to be produced. Cells obtain their energy from ATP conversion.
 Cells would normally be able to get phosphorous in the form of PO_4. Nitrites cannot be oxidized by nitrobacter into nitrates without phosphates.

ABSORPTION:

During the absorption stage, nitrogen is absorbed into the living organisms. Plants take in nitrogen in the form of nitrates through their root hairs.
 This nitrogen is processed by the plants further and used as both amino and nucleic acids.

AMMONIA:

As living organisms produce waste, decay or die off, nitrogen is converted to ammonia and is given off by the organism.
 This process is called ammonification.

DENITRIFICATION:

Occurs as nitrogen is once again recycled back to the atmosphere in the form of nitrogen. This happens when nitrates, and nitrites are converted back to the N2 gas via anaerobic bacteria.
 This completes the nitrogen cycle.

AVOID THE FOLLOWING:

Beware of using any other aquarium products like algae preservatives, water conditioners or other products that you would normally use for pet fish.

 None of these products are going to be beneficial to the mini aquaponic ecosystem that you are trying to establish.

Remember to reduce feeding as much as possible to ensure that less destructive ammonia enters the system. Ammonia substantially reduces the production of nitrites.

Leave the pH levels alone. They will automatically take care of themselves over time and should lower accordingly. You may potentially have to add certain things to maintain your pH at 7.0.

IMPORTANT POINTS TO REMEMBER

Invest in a really good quality water test kit and educate yourself as much as you can about water.

You can do this online, by asking those in the know or even reading books such as this one.

Testing the quality of your water on a regular basis is one of the few activities that will be ongoing and something that you should learn to master.

I would recommend that you look for a proper testing kit rather than trying to rely on the testing strips, as these are not always accurate and can often be difficult to read.

The only time that you should add any salt to your water at all should be during your cycling time.

This should also only occur if you are cycling with fish.

Remember that I mentioned that salt does not evaporate, so it is extremely important to add this in moderation and keep accurate notes of how much salt you are adding at a time.

Before you add your expensive fish that you plan to populate your system with, go out there and buy some cheapies that you are prepared to sacrifice if the system is not yet ready.

This decision and small exercise could end up saving you loads of money in the long run.

Something that we have not discussed up till this point, but will be hugely beneficial in giving your system a kickstart—consider adding a couple of red worms that you would normally find in composting to your plant bed once your system has cycled and you begin adding your fish.

CHAPTER 4: IDENTIFYING THE BEST FISH FOR AQUAPONICS

"O nly by adopting a mentality that focuses on maximizing conservation and ethical food production techniques, can we establish a future of production that works. We have to intensify production. But it needs intensifying the right way, not just relying on the finite resources, because in the long run it won't work. It's a false economy, we'll run out." ~ Antonia Paladino, Founder of Bioaqa, biggest integrated aquaponic trout farm in Europe

Finding the very best fish for your aquaponics system is dependent on a number of factors.

You need to consider the climate that you live in, what species of fish are actually either indigenous or common to the area, and whether you are going to settle for fish that are just decorative or whether you plan on eating them as a means of obtaining your source of protein.

This is one of the benefits of moving towards aquaponics rather than hydroponics.

There are many other differences and benefits between the two and we will list them further in this book for you to make an educated decision as to what will work best for you.

Before you should even be considering which fish are going to work best for you, think about your needs and whether you are going to buy your fish from a hatchery, a local aquarium or online. Buying fish online is now in fairly high demand and so you will probably find someone in your area who delivers directly to your door.

A small sidebar here, if you are planning on ordering your fish online, please make sure that you are there to receive them, or someone else has access to receive them.

Please remember that they are live produce and will need to get into their respective tanks as a matter of urgency.

There is no right or wrong answer when it comes to purchasing your fish—some people prefer to go to the supplier, hatchery or aquarium and select the fish that they want themselves, while others are content to accept whatever they order online.

Some of the most successful fish for aquaponics include Angelfish, Bluegill or Sea Bream, Crappie, Goldfish, Guppies, Koi, Mollies, Sunfish, Swordfish, Tetras, Tilapia, and Pacu.

Some of these are purely ornamental, while others can be reared for eating. The following fish are also widely used in aquaponics:

Barramundi, Carp, Catfish, Largemouth Bass, and Golden, Silver and Yellow Perch.

The main consideration is how well the species of fish will do within your own specific climate.

This dictates pH and water temperatures, which we will discuss a bit later—but it doesn't help bringing in a tropical fish to a climate that is not conducive to its survival. Remember that the aim is for the fish to be able to both survive and thrive.

To give you a better understanding of this, let's look at each of these fish and see what sort of conditions they need to thrive in.

ANGELFISH

If you were considering using these beautifully colored fish in your tank for aquaponics, this would definitely be an option for the ornamental variety of fish.

They can be very pretty to look at and can have a calming effect over you while your plants are being nourished, however they are not suitable for consumption at all.

Most angelfish only grow to around four to five centimeters in length, making them a small fish by comparison to a Tilapia or Largemouth Bass.

Another concern when it comes to choosing Angelfish for aquaponics is that they are extremely inbred as a species and can become prone to carry diseases around with them—this would not really make them ideal, unless you were running a pretty small unit somewhere in your home and the protein component was not an issue for you.

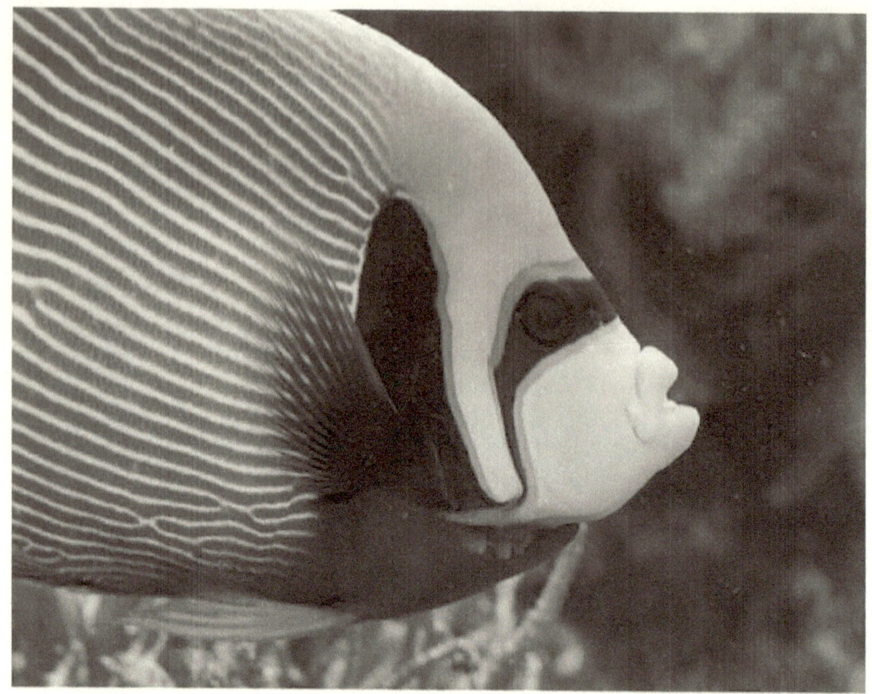

Source: Emperor Angelfish - Pixabay

BLUEGILL OR SEA BREAM

The Bluegill, also referred to as bream or sometimes even perch (which is incorrect), is a freshwater fish that can be found in North America.

It's happy to live in either shallow or deep-water conditions, which makes it great for aquaponics.

If you are planning on stocking these, it may be worthwhile to add some tree stumps or other types of structures in your ponds as they enjoy hiding in this type of environment.

They would be great to stock for protein if you were situated in North America as they can grow to a reasonable size, ranging anywhere between 12 inches (30cm) long and approximately 4½ pounds (2.0 kg) in weight.

They are omnivorous and will pretty much eat anything, which is also important when it comes to aquaponics.

With Bluegill, you could even feed them scraps and they would be quite happy.

When it comes to reproduction, Bluegills spawn between May and August each year, and water temperatures should then be between 67° – 80°F. The males will create spawning beds in shallow water and are extremely protective of these nests.

During mating, one female will choose only one male who she can spawn with, but when this is done, the male will chase her back out of the nest and then protect the young.

Smaller females can produce around 1,000 eggs at a time, while larger females can produce over 100,000 eggs.

The male will closely guard the eggs until they hatch, and the larvae are able to swim away.

The lifespan of a Bluegill is approximately four years when they reach full maturity, but others have been known to live up to eleven years.

Source: Bluegill or Sea Bream – Pixabay

CRAPPIES

There are a number of species that fall into the Crappies family. Some of these are actually Bluegills as discussed above, while others are Largemouth Bass. Crappies actually form part of the Sunfish family and are the biggest of the entire Panfish species. There are only two different types of crappies, white and black!

The White Crappie looks slightly different to the Black Crappie and although it grows to around the same size (6.7" to 20.9"), they weigh the same as the Black Crappie. While their coloring is much lighter and blotches that they have on their body often appear more like stripes, they also have only five or six dorsal fins, compared to the Black Crappie who have seven or eight. Counting the dorsal fins is actually the easiest way to tell these two apart, because while in the water, they can often appear to be exactly the same color.

BLACK CRAPPIE

The length of Black crappies can vary between 5" and 19".

The average weight is around 1⁄2 pound to a pound, although if they really get big, they could weigh in at 3 or 4 pounds. A black crappie is distinctive by its evenly spaced blotches that are located on the sides.

The white crappie is usually silvery green, while the black crappie is more olive colored.

Because crappies are extremely hardy fish, they are a great choice for starting out with aquaponics.

Ideal temperatures for crappies are between 70°-75°F, although they can still survive at temperatures as low as 55°F.

 Allowing temperatures to fall down to 55°F should be avoided as much as possible though because by this stage, the fish become lethargic and the amount of waste produced is a lot less than when water temperatures are optimal.

Crappies can even thrive in temperatures of up to 80°F.

Remember that it's not just the water temperature that affects the survival of the fish that you decide to stock, much of the success rate also depends on the pH of the water, which should ideally be between 7, and 7.5.

Source: Black Crappie - PNGKey

GOLDFISH

Goldfish make for amazing aquaponic fish, although remember that if you are going to choose to use Goldfish, these are usually just ornamental in nature and can obviously still produce hours of fun and enjoyment in being able to watch them while you unwind after a hard day's work. Some further reasons for choosing to use Goldfish to support your aquaponic system is that they are extremely hardy.

They can survive in diverse water temperatures and so this doesn't become a case of having to double check water temperature or consider which side of the continent you are living on.

Another huge benefit of using Goldfish for your system is that they produce a lot of waste, which is exactly what your plants are going to need to thrive on.

Goldfish come in two main varieties—fancy and slim-bodied.

The variety of Goldfish that you choose for your aquaponic system would depend on where you plan to build or house your system.

If you are planning on having your system outside or in a cooler environment, it is recommended that you look for the Slim-bodied Goldfish because they are hardier and less likely to survive the elements.

Some of these would include Bristol Shubunkins, Comets, Commons, Shubunkins, Wakins, and Watoni. Even outside in cooler climates these don't require a heating unit, as long as the water is not likely to freeze over.

If it does get cold enough that the water is going to freeze then you would need to shut your system down in winter.

You would need to bring whatever plants are in the tank inside as well because it will be highly unlikely that these would be able to survive the icy climate.

If your system is indoors, then Fancy Goldfish are the answer if you are after ornamental fish. They are ideal for placement where there is little to no temperature fluctuation. A great idea when it comes to using fancy goldfish are the addition of goldfish-safe snails. These speed up the process for breaking down waste, while being natural algae eaters at the same time.

If you are planning on using either of these varieties of Goldfish, the quality of the food that you are planning on giving them is extremely important. Remember that it is really going to be the waste from this food that is going to feed your plants and you want to ensure the highest quality waste will be produced.

Some problems that could arise if you feed them cheaper and lower quality food could lead to things like cloudy water and swim bladder problems, which not only affect the tank, but also the fish.

It makes perfect sense that if you are growing plants to be harvested and consumed by yourself that the quality of what is going into the fish will affect the quality of the waste by-product.

GUPPIES

While guppies would probably be the last fish that you would consider to be suited to aquaponics, they are in fact very suitable.

There are a couple of reasons why they work really well for aquaponics—firstly they are really entertaining to watch because they dart backwards and forwards really quickly, and the second reason is that they are another resilient fish.

There are several factors that you need to get right before you can proceed with guppies. You must understand their different tolerances before you include them in your aquaponic tank.
Once you understand this, you can create the best conditions in your tank for success. While they are extremely hardy and resilient, they can take work to maintain and look after some other species and you need to do your research before taking the plunge.

I bet that you never knew that there are more than 40 different species of guppy out there, some of them being the Common Guppy or the Rainbow Fish. These are available worldwide and are usually a popular choice for aquariums and aquaponics systems; Endler Guppies are related to the common guppy but are green, red and silver in color.

They love a tranquil environment and warm water. One of the most important questions that are asked when it comes to guppies is whether they can be combined with other fish.

Not always in an aquaponics setup because you need to make sure that temperature and pH are suited to the needs of the fish that you are rearing, which is seldom the case when it comes to any two varieties.

With Guppies however, they could be combined with non-aggressive fish like Catfish or Tetra. The main reason for not including them in other systems would be for the fear of inbreeding, which won't happen with these two varieties.

KOI

Source: koi-1298672_960_720Koi-Orienntal-Fish-Pixabay.jpg

Next to Tilapia, Koi are the second most popular fish that aquaponics enthusiasts' stock as their fish of choice.

The main reason for this is because they are highly suited to aquaponics tanks and setups whether indoors or outdoors.

Koi live fairly long and breed in the system. This is because as a species, Koi are used to being kept in ponds or tanks as ornamental fish all their lives.

Not that you would ever guess, but Koi are related to both the Goldfish and Carp species. Being highly resistant to diseases and most parasites, they are ideal to be kept in close surroundings with other fish.

 Because they are used to being in ponds, using Koi are best suited to an outdoor aquaponic environment.

You can even design your setup so that your Koi pond becomes the main feature in your garden. Because of their unique patterns and designs, watching Koi can prove to be both therapeutic and relaxing.

Another major benefit to stocking Koi is that they are easy to sell should you find yourself in a situation where you have too much stock.

The downside of using koi for your aquaponics fish species is that depending on where you are located in the world, you may require permits to stock them.

The best way to resolve this would be to check with either your local forests and fisheries department or the suppliers of the Koi. They should be able to provide you with this information.

Some key considerations when you have your Koi pond outdoors is that they could be prone to predators.
The best way to prevent this from happening and protecting your Koi would be to consider net covering, fencing around the pond and possibly even covers should you be aware that you have birds such as Fish Eagles in the area that could possibly endanger your fish.

MOLLIES

Source: fishy-3214876_960_720 Pixabay.jpg

Mollies are another ornamental fish that can be used for your aquaponic system. As you can see by the image, they are pretty and would be great to look at in an aquarium-based system.

It is not recommended for you to use them for any larger outdoor system where a lot of waste is needed, purely because they aren't able to produce the amount of by-product required to feed your plants sufficiently.

If you are only considering a smaller indoor system then they would be ideal and are recommended along with Goldfish and other ornamental fish.

TILAPIA

Source: tilapia-799876_960_720-Tilapia-fish-pond-Pixabay.jpg

Ask any aquaponics expert which the most popular fish is to use for their system, and they will more than likely answer 'Tilapia'. There are also many reasons why they are so widely used and popular. Some of the main reasons they work so well is because they are resilient and hardy, they can be an ideal fish to begin aquaponics with on a small scale until you are confident to move on to bigger things.

Another major plus is that they are actually quite friendly and will be friendly towards whoever feeds them. They also get on quite well with Catfish.

Tilapia are quite pleasant to the taste and grow big enough for a decent meal. They thrive in warmer water than other fish, opting for approximately 80°-86°F. They can survive fluctuating temperatures that range between 60°-95°F comfortably.

You will be able to farm Tilapia in cages, ponds or tanks without any problems. A Tilapia breeds on average every 4-6 weeks, making them a constant source of protein.

While they themselves are omnivores and only require between 22-33% protein as food, a Tilapia will grow to be approximately 600g in six to eight months.

One of the only drawbacks when it comes with farming Tilapia is that if they are in a cooler climate, you may require a heating system in your tank to keep the water temperatures within the above ranges.

If you live in an area where you need to get a permit for Tilapia, consider the Nile Tilapia rather than the Mozambique Tilapia.
 Most commercial aquaculture or aquaponics farmers have opted for the Nile Tilapia as their fish of choice.

 The main reason for this is that it has been genetically modified to yield and produce more over a shorter time frame. Evidence suggests that the Egyptians used to keep them in ponds along the Nile some 3,000 years ago, however, the records of them being used in local aquaponics only date back to around the 1980s.

CHANNEL CATFISH

These are highly recommended for larger systems. Most people use these in areas where Tilapia is illegal. They are extremely well-suited to much cooler climates. If you live in an area where your winter is colder and you are running your system outdoors, these should be your fish of choice. Because they are accustomed to being in cooler water, you don't need to invest in water heaters to keep water temperatures constant, as you would do with Tilapia.

Source: catfish-4377964_960_720Pixabay.jpg

There are a couple of pointers when it comes to rearing Channel Catfish. Firstly, they like to live at the bottom of the tank.

It is important to know this so that you don't overstock your tank or try and raise them as this will cause them to get hurt.

It's not ideal to keep them in deeper or smaller tanks. A recommendation when working with Channel Catfish would be to raise them with other fish species that mainly use the top of the tank.

These would include fish such as Tilapia, Bluegill and Perch. Because they only live at the bottom of the tank, a much larger tank is recommended, i.e. in excess of 250+ gallon.

The ideal temperature for a Channel Catfish to survive and thrive is between 75°-80°F, although they can tolerate temperatures between 40°-90°F, making them also fairly flexible in nature.

Channel Catfish grow pretty quickly and can reach maximum sizes of between 40 – 50 pounds. Although they only need 32 – 38% protein.

Their feed conversion ratio is around 2:1 (2 pounds of feed to 1-pound size fish).

Catfish can be eaten and are rich in Vitamin D.
Before eating them though you need to skin them when preparing them for cooking.

LARGEMOUTH BASS

Source: photo-1551464664-222eeb2d2034largemouth-bass-unsplash-Luis-Vidal.jpg

These fish are usually popular to North America and are known more as gamefish rather than a fish to stock for aquaponics.

Largemouth Bass are part of the freshwater fish family, making them ideal for aquaponics.

They have a very wide temperature tolerance range, which means that they can be safely bred and reared through both winter and summer months quite safely.

Their temperature tolerance ranges between 50°–86°F, although their optimum temperature is around 68°–97°F.

The Largemouth Bass is carnivorous and needs more than 40% high protein diet. You can eat Largemouth Bass.

It has white flesh and is rich in omega-3 fatty acids. The bonus of eating this fish is that it is boneless (for those like me that can't stand picking bones out of fish).

Due to its size, the Largemouth Bass does require a much larger tank – the smallest that you will get away with will be around 1200 gallons.

RAINBOW TROUT

Source: trout-277056_960_720Rainbow-Trout-Pixabay.jpg

The Rainbow Trout belongs to the Salmon family and because of this, they are not only edible, but have a really pleasant taste. Trout thrive in colder water with average temperatures ranging between 57°–60°F and minimum temperatures for survival being 50°–64°F. Trout are also carnivorous and need up to 50% high protein diet.

You can expect rapid growth amongst your Trout, they are some of the fastest growing fish of all those used for aquaponics, adding between 800 to 1000 grams every 14 to 16 months. Rainbow Trout are better suited to colder climates because they don't survive in warm waters.

Trout need clean water to thrive, unlike Tilapia. They can be quite high maintenance because you need to ensure that their water is well oxygenated at all times and that the dissolved oxygen level never drops below 5.5ppm.

Trout also like to jump, so a covering of some description on your tank is going to be a necessity. While you may have your heart set on rearing Rainbow Trout for their specific taste and flavor, the climate that they survive in leaves you only a limited variety of plants that you could grow.

Because they are carnivorous, they need to be fed commercial fish pellets, and smaller fish, flies, snails and even bloodworms.

There is also a genuine danger of them attacking and eating smaller Trout as part of their feeding routine, which would need to be closely monitored—our recommendation on trout rearing for aquaponics would be to keep them only if the climate dictates and you have sufficient experience to work with them.

They take a lot of time and effort to rear successfully.

The last two fish that we are going to discuss that could potentially work best for your aquaponic system will be the Jade Perch, and the Carp.

JADE PERCH

Here is another resilient and hardy fish that grows rapidly.

 It stems from Australia and so is used to much warmer environments.

Some interesting facts about the Perch is that they are really placid and get on well with other species, making them an ideal option for aquaponic enthusiasts where the climate is right.

Additional bonuses are that they can be harvested within about a year and they are delicious to the taste.

Another fish that is high in healthy omega 3-fish oils.

The ideal temperatures for Perch would be between 70°–80°F. It's worth mentioning that if temperatures drop below 65°F, the Perch will stop eating, could become inert and die.

As omnivores, they eat almost anything, but still need a medium protein diet. Another downside of Perch is that they won't breed while in captivity unless they are injected with a specific hormone to allow this to take place.

Being fairly peaceful, they get on well with other fish in an aquaponic system.

Even though they are resilient, they still need a fair amount of dissolved oxygen to survive.

These can easily be pumped into the tank using traditional stones and an aerator. The best pH for Perch is between 6.8 and 7.8.

Source: perch_3585165_960_720Perch-fish-Perca-Pixabay.jpeg

CARP

This would be your "go to" fish if you were planning on setting up an aquaponics system in the UK and they are ideal for larger scale aquaponic farming.

Part of the reason for this is that they have a high tolerance level for both hot and cold temperatures and can therefore survive the UK winter as well as summer conditions quite comfortably.

Carp do favor warmer temperatures and therefore a greenhouse would be ideal for them because they grow better in warmer waters.

There are a large variety of different Carp available and while they all belong to the same species, the most important three to remember would be the Common Carp, the Mirror Carp and Koi Carp.

Similar to both Tilapia and Catfish they can survive and thrive in water temperatures between 32°–90°F, although the ideal water temperature range for maximum growth is 75°–82°F.

Carp are omnivores and can survive with only medium levels of protein in their diet. They only need about 35–45% protein.

Feeding Carp pellets is a good idea, with the regime of fewer pellets but more often because they do not have a stomach to process the food. On average they would eat approximately 2% of their body weight per day.

Regular Carp - Source: animal-2029698_960_720carp Pixabay.png

Koi Carp - Source: carp-217229_960_720Carp-Koi-Pixabay.jpg

CHAPTER 5: COMMON MISTAKES IN AQUAPONICS AND HOW TO AVOID THEM

"My green thumb came as a result of mistakes I made learning to see things from the plants point of view." ~ J. Fred. Ale, posted on Instagram by Harperponics

There are a large number of very common mistakes that most people make when it comes to aquaponics.

Below is a list of those that are most common, and we are going to discuss them in greater detail so that you know exactly how to avoid them at all costs.

ENSURE THAT YOUR WATER QUALITY IS CORRECT

Avoid adding poor quality or tap water into your system at all costs unless the water has been tested and reported as being suitable. Because water is the key component ingredient to any aquaponic system, this is the very first thing that you need to get right. This is what is going to make sure that your plants receive all the nutrients that they receive to survive and thrive. And, it is also home to your fish. In a nutshell, if your fish are happy, your plants should thrive.

There are five key areas that you need to monitor for your water to be suitable and effective. These five things are:

- Your dissolved oxygen level (DO) as we have discussed above. The correct DO is actually 5mg/liter of water.
- The pH of your water should normally be around 6.0–7.0 (having said this, remember that your pH is directly linked to the requirements of your fish, so take this into consideration now as well). Does your pH match up to the pH of the fish that you are stocking?
- Your water temperature should ideally be between 64o-86oF, although, like the above comments on pH, water temperature is also directly linked to the type of fish you stock and you need to adjust your water temperatures accordingly. If your fish needs warmer temperatures, consider some form of a heating unit that can be added to your system that will raise the temperature sufficiently. Be careful not to overheat the fish tank, pond or pool either.
- Total nitrates — this is the ammonia, nitrites and nitrates.
- The final thing you need to consider is your water alkalinity.
- Chlorine, pH and parasites or pathogens also need to be checked before you even begin to use your aquaponics system. With the chlorine and fluoride content being different all over the world, it is vital to test this before simply adding your fish. This can easily be tested with a chlorine test kit. Remember that too much chlorine can be deadly for fish. Most test kits make for easy testing and you can easily diffuse water by allowing it to sit with an aeration unit running for approximately 48 to 72 hours.

ENSURE THAT YOUR FISH TO WATER RATIO IS CORRECT

Many new aquaponics enthusiasts want to grow as many fish as quickly as possible and this leads to a number of problems.

The first is an obvious one, overcrowding your tank, pool or pond. Imagine how you feel in an overcrowded train, not great! This is how your fish feel when they are squashed in a small space.

The results of overcrowding can result in losing fish because they simply cannot survive the high levels of nitrate that will be in the tank, but it can also stunt their growth, which is exactly the opposite of what you are trying to achieve.

Let's look at what too much nitrate does to a fish, and how you can avoid it or treat it if it does occur?

While ammonia poisoning is common among fish, believe it or not, nitrate poisoning is even more common.

Your entire system is likely to go into nitrate poisoning mode as soon as your nitrate level reaches or exceeds 6ppm.

This level typically occurs the moment there is more pollution in the tank than what can be handled and broken down by the beneficial bacteria.

New tanks are way more susceptible to this phenomenon, especially when they have not yet been completely colonized by the beneficial bacteria yet.

The most critical point is just before the tank is beginning to cycle. This is another reason why you need to be patient in setting up your system and make sure that you aren't too impatient to get your system up and running. There are two different strains of nitrifying bacteria.

The one that breeds, and feeds bacteria is known as nitrosomonas and these both eat the ammonia and produce nitrites.

The chemical term composition is NH3-> NO2, while the other is known as nitrospira and this converts nitrites to nitrates (NO2-> NO3).

This has slower reproduction rates and takes much more time to establish itself. Nitrate is what is needed for the plants to grow and does not have a harmful effect on the fish.

Nitrite poisoning can also occur in established systems due to overstocking of fish and overfeeding.

The most common causes of this happening are poor filter maintenance and new tank syndrome.

If you wash your grow beds, this could also result in the beneficial bacteria being washed away, causing the same symptoms. While this won't have any effect on your plants, it is deadly to your fish and could cause their death.

Remember that aerobic bacteria cannot colonize in the lower layers of the media that is dense with fish waste and muck. If oxygen levels are too low a rather nasty strain of anaerobic bacteria begins to form and thrive.

If you think of the beneficial bacteria as the engine that is running your aquaponics system, think of this particular strain of bacteria as hitting the engine into reverse at high speed! It immediately begins to once again convert the beneficial nitrates back into nitrites.

You will be able to recognize that this is starting to happen by watching the color of your fish. The moment that they start turning pink or red on the fins and tail, this is an indication that your fish is under stress due to nitrite poisoning.

Fish survive through moving their gills rapidly, as well as consuming oxygen from the surface.

You will notice that healthy fish will begin to move more rapidly around the tank when they are in a state of shock.

Fish suffering from nitrite poisoning will appear sluggish with little activity. Here are a couple of other signs that you could look out for:

- Their gills begin to move more rapidly.
- Their gills begin to turn tan or brown in color.

- They seem to be gasping for more air on the surface of the water.
- They are way more passive or limp and often remain near the water outlets.

Nitrite poisoning prevents the blood cells from carrying vital oxygen into the fish's bloodstream, often turning the bloodstream of the fish brown in color.

Because of this, the fish will become weaker and weaker, often suffocating because it simply cannot get enough oxygen from the water.

If the fish is exposed to nitrite poisoning for any length of time, its immune system becomes compromised and this allows secondary diseases to suddenly appear. Often, these are a result of bacterial infections.

You will also notice that there will be a string of fish deaths in your tank simultaneously, or directly one after another.

Make sure that your nitrite level should always be zero or really close to zero. Even levels that are 0.25mg/liter can cause some stress to species that are more sensitive.

Your nitrite levels should never exceed 0.1mg/liter.

HOW TO LOWER THE NITRITE LEVELS IN FRESH WATER

- **Add salt to your water**—by adding about half an ounce of salt per gallon of water, methemoglobin build up will be prevented. This prevents or reduces the influence of nitrite to remove oxygen from the bloodstream of your fish. While this technique has been researched and recommended that the most effective dosage is 1lb of salt to 150gal of water, you should keep an accurate record of how much salt you are adding and when, because salt does not evaporate.
- **Add bacteria**—whenever you change either the media, filter or the tank itself, it's a good idea to add some beneficial bacteria to your tank. This is easy enough to do by simply taking some of the gravel or medium from your existing tank that is running optimally. This will help to establish a new colony of beneficial bacteria fairly quickly. If you are going this route however, it's important to make sure that the gravel or grow media that you use is clean and pathogen free.
- **Don't use treatments or medications**—while it may be tempting to simply treat with chemicals, remember that many of these chemicals actually kill off the beneficial bacteria as well. This will leave your fish open to other infections and diseases such as fungus. The most important thing to do should be to make sure that your water quality is as good as possible.
- **Change the water**—changing out between 25% to 50% of the water with water that has been dechlorinated and repeating this pattern every day until the ammonia and nitrate levels are at zero is the quickest way to resolve this issue.
- **Stop feeding**—stop feeding your fish and avoid adding any new fish to your tank until the ammonia and nitrate levels return to normal.
- **Increase aeration**—this is easy enough to achieve by adding an additional aerator to the tank, aquarium or pond. Not only will the additional bubbles keep your fish alive, but it will assist your beneficial bacteria to continue to grow.
- **Clean the tank**—remove all uneaten food from the tank and make sure that the bottom of the aquarium or tank is completely free from any uneaten food that is decomposing.

While these are ways to solve your nitrite poisoning problem, prevention is always better than cure.

As suggested at the beginning of this section, there are ways to avoid nitrate poisoning.

These include avoiding overstocking, choosing fish that are not susceptible to disease, avoiding overfeeding (it's better to feed your fish in smaller doses over the course of the day, rather than a massive feed once a day).

You should also make sure that your grow beds are acting as a biofilter and are effectively removing or stripping the impurities from the water that is recirculating.

 If your water ever looks cloudy or foamy then you know that you have a problem and you should be looking at solving it as recommended above.

The water pump that you are currently using should also be able to circulate the entire volume of water in the fish tank approximately four to five times per hour.
If it is not doing this then you may require a more powerful pump.

CHOOSING THE RIGHT GROWING MEDIA

This is probably one of the most common mistakes made in aquaponics today. People make poor decisions on the growth medium that they are going to use.

Most people look for what is readily available and accessible to them, without doing the necessary research and finding out exactly what the best grow media are.

Before we go into the list of what is available it should be mentioned up front that certain grow media that are suitable for hydroponics are NOT suitable for aquaponics.

Remember that you need a grow medium that is going to support the needs of your plants, allows you the greatest yields possible and it also takes the least amount of work to maintain.

Your grow medium will also need to suit the aquaponic system that you have chosen, whether you are working with DWC or NFT or any other system, make sure that the medium is working for you and not against you.

The rule of thumb when choosing your grow medium is that it needs to be the easiest to maintain.

For example, when using the raft-based technique, all that is required are net pots that sit within the rafts themselves.

There are no right or wrong grow media, other than utilizing anything that contains soil or small particles that can be washed through the system.

The most important thing to consider should be that they meet the needs of the system that you are using to grow your plants in.

They also need to support the plants that you are growing with the main objective of keeping the roots moist, without suffocating the roots, causing oxygen deficiency, resulting in root rot.

While this disease is less common in aquaponics, it can still occur. Before embarking on your project, it's worth gathering some information on what is available, and what could potentially best meet your needs.

Here are a couple of options, along with their cost indications, pH factors and lifespan:

- Coco Fiber & Chips are low to medium priced with a neutral pH but have a short lifespan.
- Floral Foam has a low price with a neutral pH and is reusable.
- Hydroton or Leca Clay is expensive with a neutral pH and is reusable.
- Net pots are low priced and are reusable.
- Oasis Cubes is mediumly priced with a neutral pH and is reusable.
- Pine bark is low priced with a neutral pH and a short lifespan.
- Pine shavings have a low cost with a neutral pH and a very short lifespan.
- Polyurethane foam insulation is low priced with a neutral pH but has a short lifespan.
- Rice Hulls are low priced with a neutral pH and a short lifespan.
- River rock is low priced with a neutral pH and is reusable.
- Rockwool has a medium cost with a basic pH and is renewable.
- Sand is low priced with a neutral pH and is reusable but is NOT recommended for aquaponics.
- Starter plugs for seedlings are low priced and are reusable.
- Vermiculite has a medium cost with a basic pH and is reusable.
- Water absorbing polymers are low priced with a neutral pH and are reusable.

For aquaponic systems, apart from the starter plugs for growing your seedlings, it is recommended that you consider:

Growstone Substrate which is manufactured from recycled glass and is extremely lightweight.

Similar to growing rocks, they are porous and provide excellent aeration to the root zone while retaining moisture at the same time.

They can hold water up to three to four inches above the grow media, while still allowing for great drainage.

The benefits of making use of this grow media is that it is sustainable, lightweight, holds both air and water (more so than Hydroton) and the air to water ratio is a major plus factor.

On the downside they can be quite difficult to clean (although being made from glass, even if they break, they won't cut you).

Hydroton Leca Clay, aka Grow Rock is also known as expanded clay.

LECA stands for Lightweight Expanded Clay Aggregate.

These roundish shaped balls are manufactured from clay that is expanded. They are extremely porous.

Even though they are pretty lightweight, they are still heavy enough to provide support to your plants.

Because they are pH neutral, they won't release any nutrients into the water. Due to their spherical shape they don't get waterlogged and can retain oxygen.

Cleaning and sterilizing these on a large scale can take quite a bit of time and they are reasonably expensive, but when you consider the benefits of them being reusable, it makes their price worth it.
In aquaponics, using these in both the Ebb and Flow system and the drip system are highly beneficial to the plants and fish.
The benefits are that they have no additional solvents added to the clay; they are pH neutral and are reusable.
Because they are coarse, aerated and expansive clay, this acts as a great support to plants as they are trying to grow.
Working with them is extremely easy, especially when it comes to planting crops. They are not compact at all.

The disadvantages are that they drain and dry pretty quickly and you would need to make sure that your roots are not going to dry out quickly.

They are also initially quite expensive, but when you factor in the benefits, the cost is worth it.

USING HARMFUL ADDITIVES
TO LOWER THE PH

The balance and relationship between temperature and pH and fish requirements is a vital component in the success of your aquaponics system.

This area seems to catch a lot of aquaponics enthusiasts. Most individuals are too impatient in waiting for their system to be ready to cycle and try and reduce the pH using various chemicals that are available.

Some try adding acid to the system. While adding these chemicals may have the desired effect immediately, ultimately, they will destroy your plants and fish.

Do not add any chemicals to your system other than what is recommended.

Remember that the nitrification (beneficial bacteria) will reduce the pH of your system gradually over time.

This slower, gradual decrease is better for the health of your fish as well.

If you are really that impatient, consider adding a little vinegar to the water. This is another slow fix.
Keep each of the dosages small and remain patient, all good things come to those who wait!

GROWING THE WRONG PLANTS

Be aware when it comes to trying to grow plants that aren't native to your area.

Even if you manage to find seedlings at your local nursery, if the crop, cultivar or plants are not native to your environment, temperature and climate you could battle to get them growing.

Remember to also grow each plant in its correct season.

It seems as though this point is repeated throughout this book, but this speaks to its importance, make sure that your fish and plants are compatible.

Your fish should be suited to the crop that you are planning on growing. Remember that the water temperature, pH and air temperature all need to be taken into consideration when choosing your crops.

Once you get the match correct, you will have healthy, thriving and bumper crops all year round.

There are three main components that are like the three-legs of a stool in aquaponics.

When you get all three right there is perfect harmony and balance. When one of them is out, the entire system falls apart.

The three legs are: Bacteria, Fish, and Plants. On top of the seat of these three legs falls water temperature and pH.

 The reason why these two factors affect the three legs is that they affect each of the three legs in different ways.
For most fish there is a temperature range that they can function effectively in and each of these have a high and low range. Temperatures also affect the

DO (dissolved oxygen) levels as well as the toxicity of ammonia in the tank. A rise in water temperature will decrease dissolved oxygen levels but will increase ammonia levels.

TEMPERATURE CHANGES IN GROWTH CYCLES

Most plants can survive in temperatures that range between 64° to 84°F. While others prefer much cooler temperatures. We have considered temperatures with each of the cultivars discussed in Chapter 1, and the temperature requirements of each of the best fish to choose from in Chapter 4.

By matching each of these to your specific climate, your seasonal requirements and crops that are usually grown at that time of the year, you should be off to a success within no time at all.

Remember that temperatures will also be affected if you are making use of a greenhouse or growing your plants indoors.

When water temperatures become too high you could experience some of the following symptoms which result from heat stress:

- Calcium absorption could be negatively influenced.
- Lettuce plants will become elongated and seed rather than growing like conventional lettuce.
- Lowered levels of dissolved oxygen in your water.
- Plant roots will possibly turn black and die.
- Wilting leaves on your plants.
- Your plants could start to drop flowers or stop the fruiting process altogether.

Remember that water temperature is influenced by both air and humidity levels as well.

Lower water temperatures mainly have only one disadvantage when it comes to growing: Growth is stunted or you could notice that it takes a lot longer for your plants to wake up in the day.

Because nitrates are the beneficial bacteria and the nutrients that plants need, it's important to understand how this nitrogen cycle works.

Because all the nutrients that the plants are going to need are transported or distributed to the plants through the water, we need to make sure that there is enough nitrogen in the water that the plants can be sufficiently nourished and fed.

In aquaponics, this works via ammonification, assimilation and nitrification in the following ways:

When the fish excrete their waste into the water, this takes on the form of ammonia and is known as ammonification.

- The first Nitrosomonas bacteria is found in the grow medium and converts this ammonia to nitrates. A specific example of growing media for your aquaponic system could be grow rocks or gravel in your plant bed.
- Next comes the second bacteria, called Nitrobacter, which is also found in the grow medium. This converts the nitrites to nitrates.
- The final step is when the plants absorb the nutrient-rich beneficial bacteria that is in the form of nitrates.

The results of this cycling exercise are that:

- All nitrogen compounds that would normally be toxic to fish are removed from the water.
- Plants receive nutrient-rich, beneficial bacteria that will help them grow.

The cycle continues as the fish are fed on a regular basis, water is replenished as it evaporates or is taken up by the plants. Plants are harvested in their season and the cycle continues.

INCORPORATE A PEST CONTROL STRATEGY

It's not too often that your system will be affected with pests of any description.

It's still a good idea to have a pest control strategy in place should you ever need it.

One of the most important things is to check your system on a regular basis to make sure that you don't have any pests, bugs or unwelcome visitors.

Remember that using pesticides and other chemicals is a huge NO, NO when it comes to running an aquaponics system, so you need to come up with a workable alternative.

One of the best solutions is to react as quickly as you possibly can to resolve any problems that you come across, especially when it comes to pests on your plants. The ideal solution in getting rid of them is to feed them to your fish.

All those little bugs, slugs, caterpillars, and other beetles will be a tasty treat for your fish to enjoy and they are rich in protein as well.

Consider using natural predators to reduce any bugs—you may want to consider adding some beneficial bugs, beetles and spiders to your plants that will naturally ward off harmful bugs. The ladybug is an excellent example of this, they feed on aphids.

ORGANIC WATER

There are a number of organic water sprays available that could be used to control larger insect infestations without harming your plants.

Remember to make sure that they are not harmful to the beneficial bacteria, your fish, your pH levels in your pond, aquarium or tank.

This organic water will run off into your system so this should almost be a last resort scenario.

FEEDING YOUR FISH

Make sure that your fish are being fed sufficiently and at regular intervals. Some of the biggest mistakes with aquaponics are either overfeeding or under-feeding.

Fish can survive without food for up to three weeks, however you will notice changes in your system.

Remember that the whole reason for having the fish there in the first place is to provide your plants with the nutrient-rich water solution. If the fish are not producing waste, this cannot happen.

Over-feeding is just as big a concern as this could lead to the unconsumed food lying at the bottom of the aquarium, tank or pond and clogging up filters.

These filters need to be checked on a regular basis to make sure that any unwanted waste or food that hasn't been consumed is removed quickly enough.

NOT WAITING FOR YOUR SYSTEM TO CYCLE COMPLETELY

This is another very common problem when it comes to aquaponic, impatience! Remember to take the time that is necessary to set your system up properly as we have discussed in Chapter 3.

You can cycle your system with and without fish but each of the required steps need to be followed to the letter for your system to become ready.

This is the part of aquaponics that is most time-consuming. It could also be the most expensive due to the cost of losing precious fish that are placed into the system before it is ready. Rather wait it out for the beneficial bacteria to form correctly and populate within your system sufficiently.

You will only ever do this once (unless you plan to set up a second or third system). A little patience will go a long way in producing a fully functioning aquaponics system.

LACK OF OXYGEN CIRCULATION

Sufficient aeration is necessary in your aquarium, pond or tank.

The water that is there needs to be circulated sufficiently and often enough so that there is enough dissolved oxygen in the water for your fish.

The best way to do this is to make sure that the pump or aeration device that you have included to your system is the very best available and meets the needs of your setup.

If you are running a small aquarium with ornamental fish and growing your plants on your kitchen counter, it makes logical sense that you only need a small enough aquarium pump that matches its size.

If on the other hand you are running a larger pond or pool setup, the pumps that you require will need to be much bigger with the capacity to circulate the water throughout the closed circuit where your plants are.

I have already mentioned that the pumps required must be able to circulate the water throughout the system at a rate of between four and five times per hour.

If your current pump is not able to do this then you are likely to run the risk of losing both plants and fish due to oxygen deficiency.

As a side note, if you are living in a region where electricity supply is not consistent, please make sure that you have back-up pumps that can run off of batteries or that you have automated generators that can kick in should the power be interrupted for whatever reason.

CHOOSING YOUR FISH

There are many factors that come into play under this heading. We have covered each of the different fish extensively in a previous chapter, but this is another common mistake that is often made when people consider setting up their aquaponic system.

There are so many different things that you need to take into consideration when it comes to the fish that you are going to stock.

This ranges from the size of the aquarium, tank, pond or pool that you plan on using.

Are you wanting to make use of ornamental fish or do you plan on rearing the fish as a means of protein (to eat) as well? While each of these are important considerations, you also need to think about whether the fish that you are wanting to stock are suited to your specific climate.

Are they seasonal or would you be able to stock them throughout the year?

This would be the first prize naturally! Another common mistake is stocking multiple varieties of fish that don't get along with one another.

Fish can be carnivorous, omnivorous or herbivorous. Know which fish you are stocking so that you don't end up stocking carnivorous fish that are going to literally make a meal of the other fish!

The ideal when it comes to looking at what fish to stock is to consider what is native to your region.

Whichever fish are likely to survive the seasonal climate of your region with the water temperature changes through summer and winter.

These become far easier to maintain and you will save on buying expensive heating systems to increase the water temperature to make sure that your fish survive cooler months or climates.

One of the last points to mention when it comes to choosing your fish—make sure that you are stocking fish that you will eat (if you are stocking for protein purposes). Not all fish are palatable, and there's no point in breeding and rearing fish that are going to go to waste.

All that will happen in this instance is that your ponds will become overstocked and lead to disease or loss of fish due to overcrowding.

KEEPING RATIOS RIGHT:

It's extremely important to keep the correct ratio between fish and plants correct.

Overstocking fish as discussed above will cause death and open the door for disease because they will produce way too much waste.

This will have a knock-on effect on your plants by providing them with a nutrient-rich solution that is too nutrient-rich.

Just as you would experience in conventional gardening, if you over fertilize a plant it could die.

Exactly the same scenario could take place with aquaponics. It's important to try and get the balance between your plants and fish correct. This is going to take some practice.

Some ways of being able to do this is by harvesting fish, while harvesting vegetables. This is after all exactly what aquaponics is all about.

If you find that you are unable to keep these stocking levels down, then consider selling some of your fish off. This is one of the reasons for starting off small so you can get used to rotating and harvesting effectively and to meet your specific needs.

Some other ways to ensure that you can keep this system going effectively is to rotate with seedlings and fingerlings, this should give you the time that you need to allow both to grow without having an overstocking problem.

There really isn't a right or a wrong way to do this, initially it will be trial and error until you can figure out how many fish you are likely to harvest while harvesting your plants.

The final common mistake that I am going to cover is one that has already briefly been mentioned but is a critical error that will cost you in fish, will possibly cost you quite a lot of money to replace fish that die.

OVERFEEDING

It's extremely important to avoid overfeeding your fish.

Rather feed them in smaller amounts at various intervals throughout the day.

Within approximately 30 minutes of feeding your fish, remove any uneaten food from the aquarium, tank or pond. This will prevent it from beginning to decompose.

Once this remaining food begins decaying it uses up all the dissolved oxygen available to the fish and can cause disease.

Closely monitor how much food has not been eaten and you have removed from the system as additional waste—you should then try and change the following day's feed appropriately.

CHAPTER 6: ADVANCED TECHNIQUES – HOW TO LEVEL UP YOUR SYSTEM

"Achieve the greatest volume and highest quality of produce possible, while reducing operating costs, and maximizing your profitability by growing smart." ~ Tom Blout, Expert at US Hydroponic Association

THINKING OF GOING COMMERCIAL?

So you have successfully set up and got the hang of a smaller system that is able to sustain your family with regular seasonal crops and fish.

Where do you go from here? the natural progression is being able to share this with others.

Due to the current crisis when it comes to sustainable agriculture, insufficient land availability, high costs of conventional farming, high costs of labor, seeds, climate change, drought and an entire host of other challenges that threaten agriculture as we know it, aquaponics can genuinely provide an answer. Let's take a brief look at each of these challenges.

Firstly, climate change has brought about irregular seasonal changes all over the world.

The change in weather patterns is apparent and is felt globally.

Areas that were used to seasonal rainfall are now experiencing crippling drought conditions that are literally bringing the conventional crop farmer to their knees.

They are unsure as to whether or not to plant their crops because rain is not guaranteed and even a few weeks out can make all the difference for any cultivar.

Aquaponics addresses this issue because there is very little water used other than in the aquarium or pond where the fish are kept.

The plants are grown in a recirculating closed system, preventing water loss and therefore the only water that is used throughout the entire process is either via evaporation, or plant uptake. You don't even need to drain and replace water like you would in a hydroponics environment.

This system can be designed to fit into any space, making it convenient in meeting your specific requirements.

If you live in a small apartment building, you may only have the space available on a countertop for a small aquarium with ornamental fish, with the grow beds above.

Alternatively, you may live on a larger property where you have access to a greenhouse, and you are looking at upscaling your operation to become a commercial one.

The message of this chapter is that whatever space you have available, aquaponics can utilize to full capacity in the most cost-effective way possible.

You will have noticed that in one of the previous diagrams of a system that the troughs are stacked or separated above one another.

This saves space, while allowing you maximum yield for your plants. You can adopt similar systems in a greenhouse environment, interconnecting the closed-circuit pipes or adding raft systems that cover the space that you have at your disposal.

Aquaponics is sustainable because with a little training, anyone is able to do it. The most challenging part of setting up an aquaponics system is the cycling process.

Once you have managed to get this right and under your belt, there is very little work that needs to be done.

Most of this work involves monitoring your pH, water and air temperature, your fish and your plants. Pretty simple stuff when you compare it to the complexities involved in conventional agriculture and the amount of labor involved. It's no wonder that many countries are beginning to teach communities how to design, build and manage their own aquaponic systems as a means of sustainable food supply.

Communities that don't have access to regular water or power can look at adopting this method of supplying themselves with organically grown fruits, vegetables, herbs and protein in the form of fish. A reasonably small area would be able to produce enough produce to feed a community.

Conventional farming costs are extremely high when you think about all the equipment that you need to invest in to plough the land, plant seeds, irrigate the land sufficiently and then to harvest the crop once it has grown. It's not just the equipment cost that you need to take into consideration but also the cost of fuel,and labor (even seasonal labor when necessary).

All of these costs add up—compared with a smaller aquaponics system, this can be run at a fraction of the cost and once it is up and running, the operating costs are reduced.

The cost of seeds, pesticides and other chemicals required in conventional farming is exorbitantly high. In aquaponics, there are no pesticides and chemicals used whatsoever.

The only costs that you would be faced with would be your seeds, seedlings and your fish, once you have designed and set up your system.

For environments that face extreme weather conditions such as drought, deserts or land that has eroded and is non-arable, aquaponics can be a cost-effective solution. There have even been instances of large aquaponics facilities being set up in the middle of the desert, that are able to support the surrounding environment.

Additional benefits to upscaling to commercial aquaponics would be that food could be grown close to the source of consumption.

This would save time, energy and money on refrigeration, transportation and chemicals that are currently being used on the foods that we are currently purchasing from your local grocer.

By growing close to the source of consumption, you are genuinely producing vegetables, fruit, herbs and protein that is truly organic.
There have been absolutely no chemicals or additives included as part of the entire growth cycle.

INTERESTING FACTS ABOUT AQUAPONICS:

An interesting fact about aquaponics is that it can be run totally off the grid. Because running your system is so energy efficient it can very easily be run off of alternate energy sources, reducing your carbon footprint even further.

Think about installing your own solar panels, windmills or wind turbines or even a form of hydroelectric power and you are good to go.

This is great news for those areas that don't have access to regular electricity, or if you just want to be that eco-friendly enthusiast.

Water efficiency is a major bonus for aquaponics, even a large-based, commercial aquaponics system uses only 10% of the water that would be used for conventional farming.

There is no wastage of water as the system circulates water throughout and with limited evaporation, the only water that is lost is what is absorbed by each of the plants.

The system never needs to be flushed out like with a hydroponic system. Instead, there is only limited topping up of water required to the aquarium, pond, or tank where the fish are kept.

If you are operating in a greenhouse this is further reduced, and there are even pool covers that can be added to reduce the evaporation even further.

There may be a slight loss when removing any excess solid waste, but it's not really worth mentioning because it's a tiny amount of water.

Year-round growing is another major benefit to aquaponics. This is especially beneficial to those out of the way places, those regions where climates aren't always suitable for growing crops throughout the year.

Think about desert climates as well as those that have shorter seasonal growing periods for certain cultivars.

Imagine being able to grow tomatoes all year round, having delicious Trout available throughout the year.
In many of these regions finding this fresh produce was almost impossible and if so, it was extremely expensive.

Think of the costs involved in getting these herbs, vegetables, fruits and fish to these out of the way places.

 Through the solution of aquaponics many, if not all of these problems can be overcome and fresh, healthy, organic food produce can be grown, delivered and consumed very close to the source.

UNDERSTANDING FISH DISEASES:

There are three different types of stress that your fish could be subjected to and we are going to look at each of these here. They are:

1. Biological Stress
2. Chemical Stress, and
3. Physical Stress.

Each of the above can be recognized and dealt with as follows:

Biological stress—when your fish is facing biological stress there are various parasites, viral diseases, bacteria or fungi in the area that are affecting them.

These unwanted organisms are normally always around, but only become a problem as soon as the conditions for them to thrive are just right.

You will know that there's a problem with your fish if they begin to behave in the same way as if they were under physical stress.

This includes eating less or not eating at all. They visibly move from the state where they were thriving, and you can begin to see that there is a distinctive change happening.

They could also begin bumping into the walls of the aquarium, trying to escape the light because they are feeling more sensitive towards it.

Many of these symptoms will have a genuine threat for your fish.

You can sort out biological stress by adding salt to the water to help them fight off some of these unwanted diseases, however it is important to get the ratios right because too much salt can be harmful to your plants.

It's recommended that instead of adding sodium chloride to take care of the problem, look for just chlorine (but in really low doses).

It's actually the chlorine that has a positive effect on the fish and warding off this unwanted bacteria.

There are also some more plant-friendly solutions out there like magnesium chloride or potassium chloride.

These will not only benefit your fish but will keep your plants safe at the same time.

Chemical stress—is usually as a result of your water quality. If there's a problem with either ammonia or nitrites in your water, your fish are going to become stressed.

If your pH levels are low this can also place your fish under undue pressure. Remember that your nitrate levels can go up to 500-700ppm quite safely without disrupting any of your fish.

Remember to remove any unconsumed food from the tank or pond within 30minutes of feeding (every feed).

If there is a problem with your filter and it is not working sufficiently well in removing unwanted waste from the tank or pond, chemical stress is likely.

All this unwanted waste in the tank reduces the amount of dissolved oxygen (DO) in the water and your fish will soon start being oxygen deprived.

Physical Stress—is probably the most common type of stress that your fish could ever go through because there are so many external and internal factors that could apply towards the creation of physical stress.

Some of these include water temperature. Fish do not have the means to self-regulate their internal body temperature because they are cold-blooded animals.

We need to know the temperature range that our fish is going to thrive in and maintain the water temperature within those ranges to prevent them from going into shock.

Symptoms of temperature problems are very similar to those of when they are suffering from biological stress – they either stop eating completely, or the amount of food they consume will be reduced.

We need to watch for optimal thriving temperatures with our fish because they can also become more susceptible to diseases that are always present.

There are a number of other things that physically stress fish out, these are things like sudden change in light (when we turn lights on and off the fish become confused—we are telling them that it is now daytime).

If they are confused, they will start swimming into the sides of the tank. Loud noises and tapping against the tank are also a problem for your fish.

Because they hear throughout their bodies via vibrations, something as simple as tapping against the tank can sound like screaming for them, and this will set them into a state of stress.

Finally, most fish prefer to live in calm waters. Examples of these would be Perch and Tilapia.

Other fish prefer to have a form of a current available in their tank – think of any typical river fish such as Trout.

We need to think about all of these things and monitor for any undue stress that we may be causing our fish.

CHAPTER 7: MAXIMIZING YOUR SYSTEM

"You can convert 1.2kg of fish food into one kilo of fish. The lost 0.2kg dissolved into nitrogenous waste. For every kilo of fish you rear, you grow about 10kg of plants and vegetables. All of a sudden, you're producing a lot from very little." We are potentially taking a system that's evolved over millions of years and we are just copying it. While it can be seen as complex, it is incredibly simple." ~ Charlie Price, from the social enterprise Aquaponics UK

Getting an aquaponics system up and running doesn't need to be an expensive exercise.

In this chapter we are going to look at a couple of different options that you could consider as a way to get your feet wet and test the waters of aquaponics for yourself without losing out on a lot of money.

The first system we are going to consider is one that is going to be upcycled from an existing fish tank that many people already have in their homes. Side bar—when I refer to a fish tank, I am referring to a proper aquarium and not just a goldfish bowl!

The pond component in this particular exercise is an existing aquarium that houses five Goldfish.

There is a corner pump that pumps the water upwards to the "plant bed" which is another repurposed window-sill rectangular flower pot. The pot has been filled with Hydroton Grow Stones.

This becomes what is known as our grow bed. The grow bed input pipe fits snuggly into a regular aquarium filter floss.

This floss makes sure that the water flow is reduced to a gentle flow rather than flooding.

EBB AND FLOW:

This system has been designed on an **Ebb and Flow or Flood and Drain** system and has a timer.

The timer allows the water to flood the grow bed for a total time of fifteen minutes, then switches off and lets the water drain back into the fish tank.

The flooding only takes place once an hour. For this particular system, it was also equipped with artificial lighting to assist with enhancing plant growth.

 This aquarium is therefore best suited for areas that don't have much natural light. Building this system is extremely easy with a relatively low cost because most of the items necessary were already available and were modified or repurposed.

The most expensive part of setting this system up would be for the hydroton grow stones.

Remember we mentioned that these could be pricier at first, but, because they are reusable the costs are worth it.

DWC OR RAFT SYSTEM:

There are many advantages to deciding to build a **DWC** system versus an NFT system when it comes to aquaponics.

Some of these benefits are that they have an even light distribution across all of their plants, you can look at the correct temperature distribution because of the large amount of water in the system.

Other benefits include being able to care for each of your plants individually because you can get to them and last but not least, they are extremely inexpensive to build.

Let's unpack it and look at some of these benefits more closely:

Even distribution of light—because all of the plants in a deep-water culture system are on the same horizontal plane, they each have access to the same amount of light which is required for growth.

When compared with a vertical system, plants are potentially cut off from direct sunlight by some of their neighboring plants.

This can be seen by the lower plants especially and the growth of these plants are likely to be affected by reduced sunlight because as we all know, plants require sunlight for growth.

Less expensive—for a normal, conventional greenhouse you would look at spending anything upwards of US$50,000 to build and install a drip tower system rather than installing a DWC system instead.

Oxygen—raft or DWC systems ensure that the roots of the plants are always submerged in water.

This would mean that you would need to make sure that the type of plants that you are planning on growing are suited to this type of aquaponics.

Because roots are always under water, additional aeration methods should be used to increase the amount of oxygen available to both plants and fish.

This can be done reasonably easily with stronger air pumps or air mats that are added to the bottom of the tank.

When setting up your system in the first place, it is always a good idea to make sure that the air pump you are making use of is suitable for the amount of oxygen needed for your fish and plants.

Spacing of Plants—working with this method means that you can evenly space your plants to meet their specific needs. For those cultivars that need more space around them, pots can be skipped or moved around accordingly.

It becomes easier to thin out those that need to be thinned out and move those that are only beginning to grow closer together.

This versatility isn't always possible when you are using other systems.

Thermal Mass—A DWC system has approximately three times more water available to your plants than a drip tower system because of the volume of water that the troughs.
A drip tower system works with only about 18,000 liters of water, whereas a DWC unit that takes up exactly the same amount of space will hold around 66,000 liters of water.
The benefits of this additional water are that it supports water temperature fluctuations especially in cooler and warmer temperatures.

Due to the amount of water, your plants and fish are protected from major fluctuations.

Most of this protection happens around the plants where it is needed most.

CONCLUSION

As we reach the end of this book, by means of quick revision, let's go over some of the things that we have covered and that you should remember when venturing out into this fantastic hobby of aquaponics.

Firstly, decide exactly what it is that you want and make sure that you have the right amount of space available to meet your needs.

There is an old adage in the carpentry game that says measure twice and cut once—this could easily be applied to aquaponics as well. Make sure that your system is suited to the plants that you are planning on growing as well.

There are some systems that are only suited to some of the plant varieties or cultivars and more of this information can be found under each of the plant headings in Chapter 1.

Remember that there are many benefits to growing your own herbs, vegetables, plants and fish apart from saving water and energy.

You are also producing crops that are 100% organic with no chemical additives whatsoever, while reducing the time between harvesting and consumption.

This is a wonderful benefit for those growers who live in remote locations and can set up their aquaponics farms or gardens and supply to the local communities where it is difficult to reach or transport.

Often there are steroids and chemicals used to keep produce fresh for longer while it is being transported across vast areas to out of the way places.

Aquaponics provides a solution to this dilemma. Further in this chapter, we take a closer look at how many different plants, vegetables and herbs can be grown in aquaponics and what is required for them to be grown successfully.

If you are wanting to match your pH to your fish, this is where you need to study up to make sure that you are getting it right!

In Chapter 2 we discussed the various different systems with diagrams of what they look like to give you a much better indication of what system is going to work best for you.

This chapter also gives you a clear picture of where everything needs to be situated for your system to work properly.

Chapter 3 covers the nutrient cycle and understanding the important role that these nutrients play in building up your system.

It also explains why it is so vitally important to practice patience and allow your system the time to cycle properly before just rushing out, buying your fish and your plants and throwing everything together.

While it may look like it's a hobby that could be quick and easy, practicing patience is the key to setting up your system correctly.

It's getting the ammonia, nitrites and nitrates correct and making sure that the beneficial bacteria is formed properly and that your fish are going to survive and thrive, along with your plants.

On average, it could take up to three months for your system to cycle correctly before you even add your fish.

Remember to take it slowly and add only one or two fish at a time that you are prepared to sacrifice, so that you don't waste any of your expensive fish on a system that is not yet ready.

Your cycling process is going to take the most time and the most attention in this entire aquaponics journey.

This will literally set the tone for your success or failure. If you can take the time to get the very basics right and build up your beneficial bacteria colony so that it is working and functioning correctly, the rest is smooth sailing from there.

While you are cycling your system, pay special attention to your pH levels that they are aligned with both your crops that you are planning on growing, as well as the fish that you are planning on stocking. It is really that simple.

If both your fish and the plants fall within the same pH requirements, then you are all set to harvest a bumper crop at the end of the process.

When there are variations in pH levels, or you are mixing cultivars that have different pH tolerances or requirements, this is asking for headaches because changing pH levels in aquaponics is way more involved than in hydroponics.

Remember that you are running an entirely chemical free system here!

Go through the list of fish that I have given you some solid information on and make sure that the fish that you are planning on stocking are local to your region, that they are going to survive the water temperatures and if you are planning on co-stocking with companion fish, that they are fish that get along with one another and have good temperaments rather than those that could potentially eat one another, or cause one another harm.

Remember that overstocking is something that could cause your fish undue stress and you could lose fish and money that way.

Chapter 5 covers an entire host of common mistakes to be avoided from water through to dissolved oxygen levels, to pest control and feeding your fish correctly, even avoiding overfeeding and how to adjust feed levels if you find that there's a lot of food left over once you have fed your fish.

Remember that it is extremely important to clean out and remove any uneaten food thirty minutes after your fish have initially been fed.

This will prevent uneaten food from building up and decomposing into ammonia which would be extremely harmful for your fish.

At the same time, check that your filters are clean and clear at all times and working effectively.

The only way to know that this is happening is by keeping a regular check on your system to ensure that it is still functioning at an optimal level.

Oxygen in the tank needs to also be sufficient for both plants and fish.

This is achieved by making sure that the air pump is strong enough to support the system. If not, it is worth investing in one that will do the job.

Oxygen deficiency is another major obstacle that will cost you plants and fish.

The entire objective of this book is to help you avoid some of the common mistakes that are made by those venturing into aquaponics for the first time.

If you are considering moving into a commercial route with aquaponics, then Chapter 6 will be beneficial for you and provide you with much of the information that you could possibly need to decide whether this is indeed an option for you or not.

This chapter also covers a variety of fish diseases, what they look like, how to recognize if your fish are under stress and how to deal with these diseases effectively.

The aim of this chapter is to assist you in being able to recognize when your fish are under stress as soon as possible, look for potential reasons why this could be so and then come up with a workable solution to reduce the situation, or minimize the stress that the fish find themselves in as a matter of urgency.

It's also being able to recognize basic diseases that your fish could be susceptible to.

Our final chapter focuses on how to maximize your systems to work to your best advantage.

Having all this information at your fingertips right now, it's time to get out there and go and dream up the very best aquaponics system that you can that is going to meet your specific needs.

Don't just build something for the sake of building—take the time to make sure that your system is going to be exactly how you want it to be.

Remember that there will always be opportunities for you to upskill and upgrade your system as soon as you feel confident enough to do so.

Thank you for sharing this journey into the fascinating art of aquaponics with me—I wish you may hours of relaxation watching your fish and tending to your crops and may you always have a bountiful harvest of whatever plants you choose!

REFERENCES

A brief history of aquaponics. (n.d.). Retrieved from https://www.stuppy.com/aquaponics/aquaponiclearn/history/

Aquaculture North America highlights UWSP. (n.d.). Retrieved from https://www.uwsp.edu/cols-ap/aquaponics/Pages/default.aspx.

Aquaponics: Chives. (n.d.). Retrieved from https://www.aquaponicsblogspot.com/2014/10/aquaponics-chives.html?M=1

Aquasi. (2019). Carp aquaponics – A sustainable production system. Retrieved from https://www.aquapona.co.uk/carp.aquaponics/

Backyard koi pond for aquaponics. (n.d.). Retrieved from https://www.aquaponicsexposed.com/backyard-koi-pond-for-aquaponics/

Bernstein, S. (2011) Aquaponic gardening: A step-by-step guide to raising vegetables and fish together. Canada: New Society Publishing.

Bradley, K. (2014). Aquaponics: a brief history. Retrieved from https://www.milkwood.net/2014/01/20/aquaponic-a-brief-history/

Brooke, N. (n.d.) Crappie aquaponics system. Retrieved from https://www.howtoaquaponic.com/fish/crappie-aquaponics/

Brooke, N. (n.d.). Guppy aquaponics: Everything you need to know. Retrieved from https://www.howtoaquaponic.com/fish/guppy-aquaponics/

Brooke, N. (n.d.). How to grow tomatoes in aquaponics. Retrieved from https://www.howtoaquaponics.com/plants/tomatoes-aquaponics/

Brooke, N. (n.d.). How to grow watercress in aquaponics. Retrieved from https://www.howtoaquaponics.com/plants/watercress-aquaponics/

Brooke, N. (n.d.). The best plants for aquaponics systems. Retrieved from https://www.howtoaquaponics.com/plants/best-plants-for-aquaponics/

Clawson, M. (n.d.). Goldfish aquaponics: ultimate guide. Retrieved from https://puregoldfish.com/aquaponics/

Deep water culture in aquaponics. (n.d.). Retrieved from https://www.aquaponicsexposed.com/deep-water-culture-in-aquaponics/

DIY aquaponics system plans. (n.d.). Retrieved from https://www.uponics.com/aquaponics-plans/

Editorial Staff, (2019). 20+ common mistakes people make in aquaponics (& how to fix them). Retrieved from https://www.leaffin.com/mistakes-aquaponics-guideline/

Editorial Staff, (2019). How to avoid & treat nitrite poisoning in your fish tank? Retrieved from https://www.leaffin.com/avoid-treat-nitrate-poisoning-aquaponics/

Editorial Staff, (2019). How to cycle your new aquaponics system? Retrieved from https://www.leaffin.com/cycle-new-aquaponics-system/

Editorial Staff, (2019). Top 17 best growing media for hydroponics and aquaponics. Retrieved from https://www.leaffin.com/growing-media-aquaponics-hydroponics/

Editorial Staff, (2019). What are the best fish species to use in aquaponics? Retrieved from https://www.leaffin.com/aquaponic-fish/

Editorial Staff, (2019). What is the optimum range of temperature for aquaponics? Retrieved from https://www.leaffin.com/optimum-temperature-aquaponics/

Genello L. (2015). Why Tilapia? Species selection at the aquaponics project. Retrieved from http://liveablefutureblog.com/2015/01/tiapia-species-selection-aquaponics

Goering, C. (2019). Types of aquaponics designs. Retrieved from https://www.ecolifeconservation.org/updates/types-aquaponics-systems-design

James, N. (2018) Know your Tilapia strains. Retrieved from https://www.farmersweekly.co.za/animals/aquaculture/know-tilapia-strains/

James, N. (2018). The best fish species for aquaponics. Retrieved from https://www.farmersweekly.co.za/animals/aquaculture/best-fish-species/aquaponics/

Ki-moon,B. (n.d.). Quote on climate change. Retrieved from https://www.brainyquote.com/topics/sustainability-quotes/

Kirsten, B. (2014). Aquaponics: a brief history. Retrieved from https://www.milkwood.net/2014/01/20/aquaponics-a-brief-history/

Malzberg, R., Weissman, R., Fleiss, A (2018). Aquaponics: How advanced technology allows Dr. Simon Goddek to grow vegetables in the desert. Retrieved from https://www.google.com/amp/s/www.rebellionresearh.com/blog/aquaponics-how-advanced-technology-allows-dr-simon-goddek-to-grow.amp

Masterclass. (2019). What is arugula? Plus easy arugula pesto recipe. Retrieved from https://www.masterclass.com/articles/what-is-arugula-plus-easy-arugula-pesto-recipe

Nordqvist, J., Gill, K. M.D. (2018). Why everyone should eat basil. Retrieved from https://www.medicalnewstoday.com/articles/266425.php

Quotes from hydroponics and aquaponics experts. (n.d.). Retrieved from https://www.uponics.com/quotes-from-the-experts

Recommended plants and fish in aquaponics. (n.d.). Retrieved from https://www.aquaponics.com/recommended-plants-and-fish-in-aquaponics/

Sawyer, T. (2019). Aquaponic fish facts. Retrieved from https://www.theaquaponicsource.com/aquaponic-fish-facts/

Southern, A., King, W. (2017). The aquaponic farmer: a complete guide to building and operating a commercial aquaponic system. Canada: New Society Publishing.

Storey, A. (2016). How to grow mint in hydroponics – all you need to know. Retrieved from https://www.university.upstartfarmers.com/blog/how-to-grow-mint

Stout, M. (2013). The complete idiot's guide to aquaponic gardening. USA: Alpha a member of Penguin Group (USA) Inc.

University of Wisconsin Stevens Point. (n.d.). Aquaponics transforms 21st century agriculture. Retrieved from http://supportuwsp.org/aquaponics-transforms-21st-century-agriculture/

Why aquaponics? (n.d.). Retrieved from https://www.stuppy.com/aquaponiclearn/why-aquaponics/